AF825069

INFORMATIONCOMMUNICATION TECHNOLOGY AND EDUCATION

INFORMATION COMMUNICATION TECHNOLOGY AND EDUCATION

(In 5 Volumes)

Managing and Competing in the Information Age

(Volume 5)

V. C. PANDEY

© Author
All rights reserved. No part of this work may be reproduced, stored, adapted, or transmitted in any form or by any means, electronic, mechanical, photocopying, micro-filming, recording or otherwise, or translated in any language, without the prior written permission of the copyright owner and the publisher. The book is sold subject to the condition that it shall not, by way of trade or otherwise, be lent, resold, hired out, or otherwise circulated without the prior publisher's written consent in any form of binding or cover other than that in which it is published.

The views and opinions expressed in this book are author(s) own and the facts reported by them have been verified to the extent possible, and the publishers are not in any way liable for the same.

ISBN : 978-81-8205-xxx-x (Set)

ISBN : 978-81-8205-xxx-x

First Published in 2018

Published by

Isha Books
D-69, New Gupta Colony,
Near DDA Market
Delhi — 110009
Ph.: +91-9212142040

Preface

In the new digital age everything is destined to revolve around information technology, be it man or machine. Cyberspace is creating a global platform where a worldwide forum is evolving that is becoming vital to economic, social and political success. Many developing countries are in a good position to exploit the opportunities of the technology revolution and advance human development. Others face significant hurdles, lacking the kind of economic environment that encourages innovation, lacking the skills and institutions to adapt new technologies to local needs and constraints.

Effective collaborative efforts are required, involving governments, multilateral development institutions, bilateral donors, the private sector, civil society to enhance the developmental impact of new technologies. Such efforts should include transfer of technology to developing countries on concessional and preferential terms, especially technology related to knowledge-based sectors, the mobilization of resources from all sources, public and private, at the national and international levels, and promoting capacity-building.

This book comprehensively analyses the trends and challenges of the information age. Its' objective is to develop in students an understanding of strategy and competitiveness in the new economy, an ability to think strategically and make business judgements in a variety of industry contexts and a capacity to manage strategically in the new competitive arena. It discusses the skills needed to manage and the tactics needed to compete in this electronic environment. It will serve as a complete reference tool to students, policy-makers, business managers and all who concerned.

Editor

Contents

1

Information Age: Challenges and Opportunities

An important technological and economic challenge, and one that is frequently mentioned in the context of democracy, is access to the technological tools that help find information and communicate. If ICT is to be used as a democratic medium, every citizen must have easy and affordable access to ICT-enabled products. At the global level, the need for action is obvious. International negotiations affecting everyone on this planet are frequently developed in different drafts that are circulated. This has created a situation where anyone who wants to take part in the development of the global framework, including the development of ICT, must have access to ICT. At the same time, it is obvious that many of those who really need to be a part of these discussions do not have access to ICT.

One of the groups excluded from these discussions are the world's poorest countries. Their biggest problem, however, is usually not access to ICT, but the lack of capacity to process all the information to which it gives access. This is partly due to their lack of ICT infrastructure and equipment, but also to the lack of other basic resources. When looking at exclusion from an individual perspective, it becomes clear that we must go beyond the country and state perspective when addressing excluded groups. Small and medium size enterprises, small scale farmers, the unemployed, young people, ethnic minorities, and those with values difficult or impossible to assess in monetary terms, are all groups that have difficulty participating in the discussions that shape the global framework due to their exclusion. Many of these groups come from economically disadvantaged countries, but far from all. In a global society, with many challenges facing humanity, it is difficult to envisage a situation where democracy is the guiding principle without ensuring that each and everyone can make their voice heard. With ICT becoming a necessary tool for influencing and participating in the development of the policies and organisations that will shape the future, as well as a tool for sharing information between citizens, universal highspeed access must be placed high up on the international agenda.

Naturally, traditional basic needs must also be addressed. However, instead of treating access and the ability to communicate as a luxury, as is frequently the case today, it must be considered as a fundamental pillar of any serious development policy. A second, less frequently discussed but no less important challenge for democracy is linked to the rapid technological development of ICT. ICT is an integrated part of a broader technological development, including tailor-made chemicals, biotechnology, robotics, quantum computing and nanotechnology. New groundbreaking innovations can be expected to come out of research laboratories in the near future, with others already available on a large scale.

A key challenge is how to democratically aim the development of these technologies in a direction that support sustainable development. With an economy that demands fast and high rates of return, incentives increase to put new technologies on the market before properly discussing and assessing their social and environmental impact. The use of ICT could, if used in the right way, facilitate and speed up proper assessment of new technologies, as well as a broader discussion of the current technological development. Today there are good arguments for the current system from a traditional economic perspective, such as economy of scale, but for democratic reasons incentives should be considered that even out the market for other, less complex and locally developed solutions. This is not to say that centralised high-tech solutions could not have an important part to play, but that other approaches also should be encouraged in order to find sustainable solutions. The broad introduction of ICT has already fundamentally changed the ways information is used, processed and disseminated. Historically, political and economic systems used to work within a timeframe of a few years and sometimes months.

During the Industrial Age, elections and annual reports were the events around which the important decisions of modern democracies have revolved. This limited timeframe has, however, often proven inadequate to deal with many of the challenges that affect nature and future generations, especially when looking years, decades, or even centuries ahead. As ICT spreads through all levels of society, the pace of economic and political decisions has accelerated even further. Today reactions on the stock market and opinion polls pressurise many groups into using time frames of weeks, days or even hours. The introduction of information technology over the last few years has for example made it possible for global financial markets and others to react and act within minutes, or even seconds, to different events around the planet. Thus, when something happens that affects the economy, the large financial and economic actors usually react in a matter of minutes, followed by the media, then by a political decision in response to the media and pressure from different groups, followed by another market reaction, then by another media reaction.

The need for rapid response increases as the social changes accelerate and different groups try to process new information. In this situation, it is easy to portray the potential responses to the challenges in a dichotomised manner, since there is little time for reflection. This trend is frequently encouraged by the mass media, where a simple and overly dramatic approach built on familiar and well-known ideas is often considered the best. In a democratic society that must take decision regarding complex questions with far reaching consequences this is, however, a dangerous tendency, as it discourages dialogue and the understanding of different and new perspectives. Sometimes the actual social and environmental implications do not even influence the process where the different actors try to foresee the next move of the other actors without checking out what the real implications are. As the real world is influenced by the reactions on the market, political decisions and how media portray reality, today's society is in a situation where the relation between fiction and reality often are difficult to understand.

Some would even claim that it is impossible to uphold the traditional idea of a difference between the real and the virtual. ICT solutions need to be democratically encouraged so as to create a situation where actors with different perspectives can meet, and where the general public can get information about what these different groups decide upon, whilst reflecting both sides of the debate. Historically, democratic societies have been organised around certain geographical boundaries, where nations, states and corporations exist. However, modern democracy is a relatively recent invention, and has not been around for more than 200 years, even if the concept that a free people should govern itself has been in existence for more than 2000 years.

The current structure of society, including representative democracy, is something that to a great extent was created as a response to the industrialisation process that took place during the last two centuries, and was thus imposed from above on nations and states that had evolved from feudalistic concepts. Globalisation has brought many changes to current institutions. Many new challenges requiring a solution are global or regional. A large number of transnational corporations have become increasingly powerful, and may act with little concern for national borders. An increasing number of individuals are also part of different international networks, through their profession or personal interest. In many cases, traditional borders today can be said to be of little or no interest—and where there is no national context, a culture is created in which people's identity and interests do not necessarily coincide with national or local geographical boundaries. In this situation, it is not surprising that the role of the existing structures, including democratically elected governments, are now being questioned.

Importance of ICT Products

The importance of ICT products is due to two basic causes.

— Even if ICT products themselves have only a marginal environmental impact, there is a great risk that the political system and mass media will judge the whole sector as environmentally unfriendly if the sector as a whole does not have a clear environmental strategy. Thus, ICTs broader credibility is threatened.

— The rapid increase and penetration of ICT products can, if no action is taken, result in increased energy demand and bigger quantities of toxic substances. Even if these problems never reach the same magnitude as they have in other sectors, they must not be ignored as they have been so far.

This would be easier with clearer targets for energy efficiency and phase out strategies for toxic chemicals used in production. In order to address the issue of sustainability, the sustainable approach must be integrated throughout the entire life cycle of every new product. Low energy use and the no use of toxic substances should be goals that are encouraged from R&D right through to the final act of recycling a product. In a networked society where hierarchies and responsibilities are often not so simple, combined with rapid technological development, central solutions cannot always be waited upon. Instead, each person involved in interaction with a product should be encouraged to improve sustainability performance. Many ICT products themselves are very small, but they are numerous.

In many cases they have significant ecological baggage, i.e. having created large amounts of waste from the creation of their basic materials through to their production. The cost of solving these problems are, however, small when compared to the overall cost for most ICT products. The ICT sector could therefore play an important leading role when it comes to, energy efficiency, sustainable production and the use of nontoxic materials. One area where ICT can contribute significantly in the short to medium term relates to the transport of goods. It is clear that ICT can be used to find more optimal transport routes and keep track of large fleets of vehicles. At first, this would appear to be positive contribution, but it could also result in further investment in a system that is inherently unsustainable. Due care must therefore be taken in order to avoid a situation where investments only result in marginal short term reductions and create an infrastructure that makes it hard to reach the necessary long term solutions.

Physical transport of a product always results in environmental degradation. The biggest environmental challenge today in the field of transport is probably the use of fossil fuel, but even with sustainable energy sources, transportation will come with an environmental cost in terms of energy use and resource consumption. A second inherent problem with physical transport is land use. As soon as goods are moved, there is a renewed demand for space, both for the vehicles to travel on and for the storage of the products. When considering a sustainable transportation system, it is important therefore to always think in terms of service. This process, along with the encouragement of local production, could set in place a less ecologically damaging economy.

Already some sectors have started a process towards a 'smart cookie business', i.e. a business built around the concept of trading and exchanging 'recipes', instead of actual 'cookies' thus allowing the product to be made locally. As there will always be a need for the transportation of some goods, there is a clear need to improve the quality of transportation. There is today a rough correlation between the level of environmental impact, and the speed with which goods are transported. This is rarely shown in the price of the product, nor is the environmental impact of the chosen way of transport. By introducing systems where the customer could choose the mode of transportation according to its environmental impact, there would be greater incentives for a sustainable transport system. One strategic area where more advanced technology already exists, and where there could be a rapid and important shift towards sustainability, is business travel. Not only would a reduction in business travel result in significant environmental gains; but done in the right way it could also contribute to a corporate culture where physical transport would be an option to be avoided if possible.

Increased use of ICT would most certainly be an improvement to today's economy. Introducing ICT would make the economy more efficient in a number of ways; more accurate estimation of demand, the optimisation of production processes and facilitated updates of products. However, very little indicates that these improvements, sometimes called eco-efficiency, would be sufficient to reduce overall resource and energy use. Efficiency gains so far have been balanced, in most cases, by increased production and consumption by those already consuming a disproportionately large share of the planets resources. If the existing pattern where mankind's ecological footprint is increasing and the differences in society are dramatically increasing is to change, perspectives must also change.

The first issue to be addressed is the very different economic and social situations on the planet. For the first time in history, a significant proportion of the world's population is living a life without material scarcity. At the same time, a much larger proportion is still living in poverty. By using the same development model for both systems, many of the negative trends seem to be accelerating instead of reversing. Solving this challenge requires elaborating solutions for the more affluent parts of the globe to shift their economies from growth economies to quality economies, keeping sustainable development in focus instead of the old economic indicators. This transformation should take into account that the poorer parts of the world need basic goods and services, such as food, transportation, communication, medicine and housing. By shifting the research and production patterns in the more developed economies, a situation would be created which would facilitate a jump forward for the poor countries, over the resource-intensive industrial society, and straight into a post-industrial society with low environmental impact.

From the customers' perspective, ICT could be used to find the product that is most environmentally friendly for the specific situation. This of course requires that companies make available information about the environmental performance of their products on the Internet. As the amount of information freely available continues to increase, there will be a need for tools that help to identify sustainable solutions, for example 'intelligent agents'; programmes that help to search for specific information on the Internet. By introducing environmental and social parameters, these agents could help users to find products and producers that supply sustainable solutions to different needs. If these agents could be tailor made to fit different needs, they could play an important part in increasing the level of sustainable development. Although many new technical solutions will be created in the future, the most important development from a sustainable perceptive would be if ICT could contribute to a society that focused less on people as consumers, and more on their role as citizens.

ICT-systems should therefore encourage the distribution of free information, whilst being developed to leave room for dreams and visions. Looking ahead, many of today's trends show that the exploitation of natural areas will continue. Resources required for the poor of the world, growing urban sprawl, increased transport, and the larger ecological footprints of more affluent societies all contribute to a situation where a minimal part of Nature is beyond immediate danger of exploitation. In order to address this issue a multi-prong strategy is required, wherein ICT could play a significant role. Transportation and consumption have already been discussed, but there are many more gains that can be made in the field of sustainable land use.

First, ICT can help monitor land use in a more efficient manner than is currently the standard. Satellites and probes in remote areas can help to understand and identify different threats, such as illegal cutting of forests. Geographical Information Systems (GIS) may also be used to optimise land use in different areas. Second, ICT can be used to communicate not only the threats to, but also the beauty of untouched areas. New technologies could be developed that would make it possible to follow life in remote areas from anywhere on the planet, which would improve personal identification with Nature and its values, such as those that exist in remote places like Antarctica, the coral reefs and the untouched rainforests. ICT can also be used for more direct educational purposes, such as calculating and communicating the footprints left by various lifestyles in different parts of the world. This helps to determine different ways of reducing society's ecological footprints, and aids the realisation that high quality life can be combined with a small footprint. With ICT, strategies to align local, regional, national and international conservation work could also be further developed, which would make all of these far more effective on a global scale.

With ICT and genetically modified organisms (GMOs) already available, difficult ethical, environmental and economic questions beg to be discussed. Much indicates that ethical questions regarding new technologies will be even more important in the years to come, as there will probably be new breakthroughs in areas such as biotechnology, nanotechnology, robotics and quantum computing. If these technologies, and especially the combination of these technologies, are to be used in a responsible way, and if technological development is to contribute solving at least some of the challenges faced today, there is a clear need to approach the issue in a strategic way. Today, whilst many products are developed only for the richest parts of society, this is partly due to the type of economic structures, including business models that have been created over time. These structures are often built around the idea of a large-scale production system, where the market consists only of a high or medium-income population. This system therefore tends to exclude many parts of the worlds population and ecology that really need the help of the newest technologies.

In order to direct ICT and broader technological development in a sustainable direction, independent agencies should be created on both the national and international level to evaluate emerging technologies. One way to address this issue would be to develop an International Convention on New Technologies, to assess the societal and political implications of emerging technologies before their commercial release. Today a digital divide, both within and between countries, is growing. This divide is a serious issue, as it tends to increase already existing gaps, making the poor on this planet even more isolated than before. At the same time, most new ICT-technologies are built around new principles such as decentralisation and flexibility, all principles that make leapfrogging over stages of development easier.

Digital Trends

New information and communicaticn technology and its applications provide developing countries with the ability to perform a kind of 'technological leapfrogging' that could enable them to reach the connection capacity required for the information networks far more rapidly. Similar forms of leapfrogging might also enable economies with a high level of skilled labour to switch to 'value-added' economies. An increasing number of states share the latter point of view and have opted for the most advanced forms of technology to implement or renew their communication infrastructures. On the one hand they have adopted policies of adaptation and technological transfer by offering attractive subcontracting capabilities, thereby relocating communication multinationals; on the other hand, they are investing in communication programmes or setting up new communication infrastructures.

Other countries, particularly in South-East Asia, have achieved something of a feat in telecommunications and the audiovisual field. Some of these nations even form the driving force for economic expansion that counterbalances the climate of recession elsewhere in the world. South-East Asia currently enjoys the highest rate of economic growth worldwide and operates as an accelerator for the whole continent: 11 per cent per year since 1983 compared with a global growth rate of 6 per cent. Its telecommunication equipment population is now close to that of the industrialized countries and in some areas is even a length ahead of European states. China, India and several countries in South-East Asia have launched their own satellites. Nevertheless, it would probably be a mistake to think that all developing countries could automatically attain this level of development.

The countries in this region of the world find themselves in widely differing economic situations as a result of a series of factors, the most important of which are the ability to attract investment, the educational level of the population, the economic policies adopted by their leaders and, finally, their cooperation with the industrialised countries and the impact of all these factors on new information and communication technology and its applications. In fact, most of the developing countries are confronted with economic and political alternatives of a strategic nature, but also with constraints and obstacles that they will have to overcome or manage if in the future they wish to set up gateways with the networks and services promised by the information society. These obstacles are financial, technical and political in nature.

Since the technical capabilities and possibilities of planetary networks, the most well-known of which is the Internet, seem closest to the idea of open, limitless communication. It is also a practical, economical solution for developing countries if they wish to have access to a universal system of communication that can make good a number of deficiencies, notably in terms of point-to-point communication. The capability of developing countries to adopt an overall strategy that links the transfer of information and communication technology to a training and research policy. Access to know-how and training in every country is a major priority. The acquisition of know-how and knowledge, which today fill the role played first by landownership and later by capital in transforming modern society, has become a priority in national development strategies. New information and communication technology is seen as an important means of completing and consolidating the traditional techniques of teaching and learning.

Virtually everywhere around the world, development programmes are making increasing use of satellite television, telematics, and even video-conferences in education, health, family planning and community development. The technology permits transmission throughout the national territory of adult training programmes and distance learning courses tailored to suit all kinds of publics. The technology offers immense possibilities for reaching vast numbers of people, with more efficient and attractive teaching methods than those used in traditional education. In addition to these advantages, if the various costs of training, such as travel in developing countries between badly-serviced rural areas are taken into account, distance learning based on new technology seems particularly cost-effective, and will become even more so as its use develops. In the medical field, new technology such as picture phoning, video-conferences and medical encyclopedias on CD-ROM are responding increasingly to a demand which already exists at the experimental level.

In a few years, doctors, hospitals, laboratories and universities will be networked and capable of telemonitoring diagnoses, analyses and examinations transmitted from one end of the world to the other in record time, via computer and video systems. Examples of experimental applications are already on the increase, notably between hospitals in developed countries. It is not enough to buy technology to gain access to the information society, however, nor should a straightforward purchase be seen as a miraculous solution. Access entails a considerable degree of effort, information, learning and popularization that developing countries will have to uphold if they wish to benefit from technological change and have the tools necessary for their autonomy, namely new information and communication technology. Nor should the latter be seen as some sort of magic wand far removed from the socioeconomic facts of life of the countries into which they are introduced.

The technology concerns every kind of user: researchers, academics, students, company executives, etc., who have to adapt to their new environment and learn to use their navigation system properly in order to optimize its potential. In addition and in parallel to this, technology transfer has to be supported by a research drive. This consists, first of all, in analysing the breakthroughs made in information technology, the conditions permitting its transfer, and its interaction with the local socioeconomic environment, and discovering the ways in which all these factors occur and interrelate. The result will be a clearer understanding not only of the use of technology, its effects, and the economic and technical constraints, but also of its advantages and the room for manoeuvre in its application. Within this global framework, research can provide a genuine form of 'strategic surveillance' used to guide policy-making by developing countries with respect to technological options.

Many developing countries since their independence have built highly diversified industrial tools in the field of communication systems, while remaining technologically dependent on supplier countries. They often find themselves confronted with R&D issues designed, driven and developed in industrialized countries. The latter have taken the high ground in the field of new technology—or are seeking to do so—by developing scientific research, taking the view that the capability to appropriate and assimilate technology depends on the degree of mastery and development attained in the strategic sector of research and development, a branch of activity in which the most advanced countries have dominant positions. The issue of international co-operation in the field of communication. The balance sheet, after several decades of international co-operation for development purposes, is disappointing.

On the one hand, it shows that very few countries have entered the newly industrialized country category, and that the use of traditional methods of development aid to enhance economic growth must be re-examined. The efforts made by the international community must be upheld and widened to include other underprivileged regions around the world, through a different approach to co-operation. In concerted fashion, this must include international organizations in order to facilitate partnership agreements with the private sector, include professional skills and ensure marketing and management know-how, and enhance understanding and knowledge with respect to the new legislation on the independent written press and the audiovisual field—in short, a different conception of co-operation altogether, leading to an authentic transfer of knowledge, in a spirit of balanced interests, solidarity and sharing.

ICTs and Digital Divide

ICT is not just another sector of economic development, nor can it simply be looked upon as a set of tools. Instead, ICT permeates every aspect of today's societal activity. Ironically, the very factors that have phenomenally improved productivity by intelligent use of the technology, also risk driving the poor to the periphery, thus creating barriers within and between societies, and could lead to social unrest and tension. Countries and people lacking capacity for ICT will be marginalized in the new economy. New trade barriers will be erected. Moreover, without access to ICT, countries will not be able to benefit from the many innovative ways of addressing poverty and basic needs that these technologies offer. One reason why the information gap is widening is that the potential of ICT in social and economic development has not been fully understood. There are still too many people in key positions in governments and aid agencies who seem to believe that only when basic needs are met does technology have a role to play. If they were right most of the poor would have to wait forever.

The issue is not about a trade-off between one or the other, but an understanding that these must go hand in hand. However, technology alone is not enough. Technology must be applied within its social context and that, in many countries, is providing a real challenge. One thing is clear. The new technologies, notably ICT, will bring about major transformations in society. The structural logic of the information society will be vastly different from that of the industrial society. Information leaks so easily that it is much harder to hide and to hoard than tangible resources were. The spread of knowledge empowers the many, by eroding the influence that once empowered the few who were 'in the know'. Information cannot be owned, only its delivery service can. And giving or selling information don't give rise to 'exchange' transactions; they are acts of sharing.

The ICT revolution by itself offers fascinating possibilities for enhancing energy and resource efficiency and reducing pollution. When society becomes more digital, the possibilities for major structural change and efficiency gains multiply. New avenues open up. Concepts such as dematerialisation, teleworking, tele-conferencing, distance education, the flexible office, e-Commerce all promise great leaps forward in terms of enhanced resource efficiency. Environmentally sound technologies (ESTs) often depend on sophisticated measuring devices, data transmission networks and automatic data processing equipment. This can be provided by ICT, thus bringing about more efficient production processes as well as greatly enhanced product performance. Moreover, with advanced communications many conventional products will be transformed into services. A newspaper becomes an on-line news service; an instruction manual becomes an interactive technical advice service; cinema film reproduction becomes a 'video-on-demand' service in the home, etc.

It appears obvious to us that a high-tech economy based on knowledge, skills and innovation ought to be a cleaner, greener economy. But few attempts have been made to assess specifically to what extent the digital revolution and the sustainable development agenda complement each other. In some areas developments so far have been disappointing. For instance, as long as e-Commerce is a marginal phenomenon in society, demand for transportation seems to increase, not the opposite. When more and more people will shop on the Net, things will change. The main reason is economics. When volumes increase it will be good business to organize transport and logistics in the most efficient way. As a result the environment will benefit.

The reader may find that most of what ICT can offer in terms of enhanced energy and resource efficiency are relevant examples only in the context of OECD countries. Activities such as telework, e-Commerce, on-line services were pioneered in the US, Japan and Europe. But there is no reason why such activities should not start penetrating countries of the South as well. In fact, they already have. Many people do not realize that China is the single biggest market for mobile phones in the world today. As the volume of foreign direct investments in developing countries has multiplied in recent years, the result will be an increased transfer of high-tech from OECD countries to developing countries. True, private investments in the South are concentrated to a limited number of countries. The challenge is to include more countries in this process, and to focus specifically on applications that would promote sustainable development.

Traditionally it was accepted that economic growth, as measured by GDP, was inevitably linked to growing demand for raw materials and energy as well as the negative consequences of pollution. If such linkages were to last long into the future the overall consequences for mankind would be disastrous. There are already clear signs that pollution levels are exceeding the absorption capacity of the global ecosystem. Climate change is the most obvious example but there are others. Parallel to excessive pollution levels, the pressures on forests, farmland, fresh water resources and fisheries are mounting. Efforts to try to de-link GDP growth and demand for energy and materials have therefore become a priority for policymakers in several OECD countries. The achievements are still limited, but there are signs of progress. For instance, the energy intensity of OECD countries has been reduced in the recent past. This is the result of a shift towards more energy-efficient technologies and less energy-intensive materials.

Scientists claim that this trend will continue, as a gradual saturation of traditional consumer goods will take place. One obvious reason is the move into the information economy. In such an economy an increasing part of transactions will be immaterial. Many products will be turned into services, which depend less on energy and material throughput. Long-term studies of energy-intensity in several countries indicate that economies use more energy per unit of output during the early phases of development, reach a peak, and then start to decrease. Liberalization and information technologies should allow knowledge to be transferred more easily, enabling emerging economies to climb the so-called energy and technology ladders more quickly. This means that latecomers ought to be able to avoid the peak in energy demand by benefiting from more modern methods of manufacturing and more efficient energy technologies. However, there are many barriers to overcome for such change to happen.

In order for the necessary transformation to more efficient and environmentally sound technologies to happen in developing countries, several barriers to change have to be tackled. Most important is to address the capacity needs. While much knowledge for improved problem-solving is now available in many scientific and engineering institutions around the world, very little of that know-how is geared specifically to addressing development and environment needs in developing countries. Most of these countries lack the scientific institutions and infrastructure to adapt and expand on new knowledge and discoveries in order to make them applicable to their local needs. In most countries energy distribution, public transport, waste management etc. are considered to be public services. Increasingly, public authorities are choosing to delegate the operation and management of public services to the private sector. If and when this happens, it is crucial that the necessary regulatory framework is in place to guarantee environmental quality. To create an adequate legislative and regulatory framework for the protection of the environment is a difficult process in any country. This is particularly true for most developing countries, where government structures are weak. Governments need to implement fiscal and regulatory policies that encourage innovation and provide direct incentives to companies that develop or disseminate technologies that contribute to sustainable development.

Fiscal incentives should also be used to stimulate businesses and households to purchase such technologies. Parallel to that, subsidies in support of fossil fuels and other technologies that are harmful to the environment should be dismantled. As already stressed, the strengthening of institutional and human capacities is a primary prerequisite for ESTs to become a priority in the development process of developing countries. The same is true for most development co-operation agencies. Technology co-operation in the field of environmentally sound technologies to the European Parliament by IED the authors conclude that a review of organisational structures and portfolios of bilateral and multilateral co-operation agencies and banks shows that there are grossly insufficient human capacities in the areas of energy co-operation. If ESTs are to become a priority of development co-operation, the institutions of international co-operation must first and foremost be given the means to understand the issues and to formulate.

The Human Development Report 2001 'Making New Technologies Work for Human Development' is one example. The emphasizes the crucial relationship that exists between science, knowledge and human capacity in addressing issues of sustainable development. One important message from the Human Development Report is that technological progress and knowledge applications are key drivers of economic growth. The logical conclusion is that support to science and technology ought to become a top priority for development co-operation. The little attention given by ODA, so far, to science and technology also means that support to ESTs have been largely neglected.

Today, village computer centers in developing countries help farmers check the going prices for their produce in the city, thus avoiding arbitrary mark-ups by middlemen. The same centers provide distance education and learning and help improve health services. Today, rural artists and craftsmen in remote villages can reach a global market with their products, thanks to non-profit Internet sites. Yet, at the same time, billions of people still live untouched by the digital revolution. Only about 7% of the world's population can claim connectivity, and the greater majority of these are living in the developed countries. As a result, the income gap between the developed and developing countries is being further aggravated by the digital divide. This holds ominous consequences for the developing countries in terms of increased poverty, unemployment and underdevelopment. This is not the result of some conspiracy against the poor. Rather it is the result of a development where access to information and knowledge are becoming the most important factors of production. Those with access to information and technology naturally benefit in this situation; those withoutaccess become further marginalised. However, the situation should not be regarded as hopeless. Even if the information revolution so far is widening the gap between the rich and the poor, this need not become a pattern for the future.

There are many tangible examples from around the world of how ICTs are being deployed to address important development goals. Evidence shows that ICT initiatives need not be confined to countries with high per capita incomes, well-developed infrastructures and high levels of venture capital in order to succeed. Indeed, remarkable progress is evident where some of these elements have been lacking. The experiences of a few countries, including both developing countries and transition economies, have demonstrated that bold actions in bringing their countries into the digital age have paid off and brought tangible results in economic, social and political terms.

Costa Rica attributes much of its recent economic growth to the widespread adaptation of ICT. The focus has been on the educational sector. Computer laboratories were installed in all of the country 's public high schools, thereby reaching 50 per cent of the children enrolled in public schools. 'Smart cards' have been introduced nationwide in public administration, transportation, public telephones and health services. Parallel to that a variety of efforts have been made to use ICT to help integrate isolated rural populations, notably by introducing multipurpose/multimedia mobile units that can be taken to any rural community and provide a variety of functions (Internet access, ICT training, e-mail facilities etc.).

Today, the country has one of the highest degrees of connectivity in Europe. All schools have been connected to the Internet; more than 80 per cent of bank transfers are made over the Internet; "smart cards "were introduced for interaction with government services etc. The per capita income has risen from US 600 in 1991 to more than US 5000 in 2000, a development largely made possible by the very proactive ICT strategy. pursued. Mauritius adopted a National Information Technology Strategy Plan early on. The primary objectives were to bring Government closer to the people through e-Government, to use ICT to enhance the education system and the service sector, and to improve the efficiency of the public sector. A special Ministry was created to promote ICT applications in different sectors of the Mauritian society. As a result of the dedicated efforts Mauritius has attracted a great number of smali and medium-sized ICT-based companies. The great majority of developing countries, however, have done little in terms of a coherent strategy to embrace the ICT revolution. This does not mean that nothing is happening in all these countries in terms of ICT for development. There are numerous initiatives, mainly among NGOs, that hopefully will help raise awareness and demonstrate, to governments as well as aid agencies, the great opportunities that the new technologies offer both for accelerating economic development and, more specifically, to help advance the human development agenda.

Small-scale enterprises and service companies have a key role to play in developing and disseminating technology. Smaller companies in developing countries often experience difficulties to obtain financing. They are either too large for micro-credits, too small to qualify for project financing or perceived as too much of a risk for commercial loans. Strategies for providing funding to small private businesses need to be developed. The international community should play a central role in assisting development country governments in pursuing the goal of Digital Opportunities for all and to support green technology leapfrogging. The following priority actions ought to be considered:

— Support to national eStrategies, based on broad stakeholder dialogues. These strategies should include the development of regulatory and policy frameworks so as to improve competition in telecommunications and the provision of IT services to the public.

— Support for the establishment of community access points in all developing countries. The goal should be that all communities in the developing world should be connected before the end of 2004.

— Promotion of ICT dissemination among children in developing countries, notably by connecting schools and educational facilities.To be effective, such a program must be complemented by adequate teacher training.

— Support for university-based centres and research networks, focussing on research and learning at the intersection of ICT and development. Special attention should be given to content building within areas like tele-medicine, distance education, democracy and participation etc.

— Strengthen efforts to mobilize public and private support for improvements of basic ICT infrastructure in developing countries. Sufficient ODA funds -a combination of grants and soft loans -must be raised to cover political and financial risks and to guarantee connectivity in remote areas.

— Support to national strategies for sustainable energy, i.e. strategies based on energy efficiency and renewable.

— Support to capacity building within developing country governments for sustainable energy; the same capacity needs in donor agencies and development banks must also be addressed.

— Before 2010, reduce by half the number of people without access to modern energy services, notably through investments in renewable energy. This would require a crash programme in terms of donor assistance. Priority should be given to small-scale projects that meet local needs, and on leveraging private finance.

— The development of renewables should be strengthened through focussed R&D efforts and public procurement, thereby driving down the costs of ESTs.

— Launching of a special programme to promote renewable energy systems in remote locations to which traditional grid-based infrastructure does not reach. In such locations solar-based systems can be the only cost-effective option. Through such solutions, vital energy needs like lighting, refrigeration, etc, as well as ICT connectivity can be met.

— Encourage the use of Export-Credit Agencies to promote investments in ICT infrastructure as well as in energy efficiency and renewables.

— Make sure that access to modern energy services becomes part of developing country poverty eradication strategies.

— Promoting debt swaps, by making money made available through the HIPC initiative to support the implementation of technology development programmes.

— Promoting new international centres of excellence in research in technologies for sustainable development.

Challenges of Online Environment

The on-line environment has now become a rapidly expanding international medium in which literally millions of users are providing and accessing content on a daily basis. For this reason the Internet offers unprecedented variety and quantity of content that is continuously changing as content is added, updated and moved around the world. As no single entity controls the operation of the Internet or the material available on it, it is impossible to form a picture at any point in time of what exactly the Internet looks like, its size or the quality or quantity of content available.

Content accessible on the Internet is stored in thousands of linked computers and is equally available by and from governments, corporations, interest groups, institutions and individuals from anywhere around the world. At present most of this content is provided free of charge. Whilst material can be accessed from any computer connected to the network, it is important to note that the content may be actually stored on a number of different computers or 'servers', which need not be in the same jurisdiction as the person accessing or creating the material. In order to understand the nature of the Internet it is useful to identify the functions which are being performed by those who are participating in the medium. These functions include providing content, accessing content, connecting others to the network and/or providing the telecommunications infrastructure. However, it is important to recognise that, unlike traditional broadcasting and publication models where the roles of content providers, publishers and viewers tend to be fairly fixed, the activities being performed by a participant on the Internet often encompass more than one function and many participants perform different functions at different times.

Of all the functions being performed in the on-line environment the distinction between 'users' and 'content providers' may be the most blurred. This is because any person or organisation can access and/or add to content available at any time. For example, a person can read and send text to a newsgroup or mailing list, create a web site or browse and retrieve information, all of which may occur in the same Internet session. Accordingly, drawing a distinction between accessing content and providing content is more a theoretical construct that usefully describes the two separate functions, which are often performed by the same participant in the on-line environment.

The term 'user' is generally used to refer to a consumer of on-line services who accesses material available on-line, typically via a link with the network through a service provider. A 'content provider' is described as a person or organisation which provides content in the on-line environment. Content may comprise text, data, still graphics, audio, video, computer programs or a combination of all of these. Organisations and individuals who provide access to on-line services to other users and content providers are referred to as 'service providers'. This incorporates those who merely provide access to the computer network which makes up the Internet, sometimes called 'access providers', as well as those who provide access along with additional services to their clients, such as assisting clients to transform content into an attractive format display on the world wide web, facilitating easy access to new and/or interesting sites and help desk facilities. Service providers range in size from individuals to small businesses, universities, government corporations and multinational organisations with operations in several countries.

Service providers usually provide their clients with 'space' to store content, such as web sites, on their computers, which are sometimes called 'servers'. This enables their clients to create and provide Internet content which can be accessed by other Internet users. Different service providers have different policies regarding the material which their clients provide and store on their servers. Some service providers requiring content providers to meet certain standards, whilst others do not wish to concern themselves with the nature of content at all. Some service providers also temporarily store or 'cache' popular Internet content from remote computers onto their servers in order to facilitate faster and more efficient access to this material for their users.

Service providers who provide access to the Internet operate as part of a network of computers. Accordingly, they enable users to access content contained on their own servers, as well as material held on the network of computers which make up the Internet, which may be stored on computers within the country in which the service providers operate, or on other computers around the world. Due to the vast amounts of Internet content which can be accessed from computers all around the world, along with the fact that Internet content is constantly changing, service providers are often not aware of, and are not in a position to be aware of, most of the material which can be accessed by those who use their service.

Encryption transfers and the use of alternative routes and protocols further exacerbates this issue and renders the blocking of even those sites which have been identified extremely problematic. The network infrastructure necessary to support on-line services in any country is usually provided by telecommunication carriers. On-line service providers usually lease telephone and data line capacity directly from the network infrastructure providers, or from 'resellers'. The potential uses and opportunities presented by the Internet for enhancing the way we communicate and access information, educational and entertainment resources appear to be unlimited. Some of the major modes of communication presently available on the Internet include e-mail, newsgroups, the World Wide Web, Internet Relay Chat, voice and teleconferencing facilities to name only a few. Each of these services can be used for a wide range of purposes and each uses its own set of technical protocols. Given the extremely dynamic nature of the Internet, it is highly likely that the range and nature of the services available throughout the medium will continue to develop at a rapid rate. From the time the Internet was first developed it has been used for virtually all forms of communication, from one-to-one communications to one-to-many communications. Forums also exist for group discussions in real time, as well as over time.

One of the main methods of communications is Electronic mail, or e-mail as it is widely known. E-mail allows users to send text messages and files to one another via personal computers. Its popularity stems from convenience, speed of delivery and low cost, as well as the capacity to reach millions of people throughout the world. In addition, the ability to transmit files of information in the form of documents, spreadsheets, graphics, sounds and computer programs as attachments to messages makes e-mail a powerful application. E-mail is increasingly being used as a mainstream form of communication for individuals, governments, educational bodies and industry.

E-mail messages are most often used for private communication, as they are addressed to an individual person or group of named individuals. In this respect, e-mail can perform a similar function to letters, faxes and telephone calls. E-mail messages can also be sent to groups of people who are members of mailing lists. These lists are usually maintained on specific computers to which individuals can subscribe by submitting their e-mail addresses. While some mailing lists are not controlled in any way, others are supervised in that each message sent to the list is reviewed by a moderator who then decides whether to allow the message to be sent on to members.

Similarly, the acceptance of new members to a list may be controlled by a moderator. An e-mail can also serve as a form of identification when a person subscribes to additional services or seeks to access content from other computers. However, it is important to note that e-mail addresses need not reflect the actual name of any given person or organisation and a person may have several e-mail addresses and/or use pseudonyms or aliases in their on-line communications. Usenet 'newsgroups' are another popular mode of communication. The term 'newsgroups' generally refers to a world wide distributed system of discussion fora. Fora have been set up on virtually every topic imaginable and users whose service provider subscribes to a particular 'newsgroup' can access and participate in these open group discussions. Messages are posted onto news servers which are distributed to other news servers around the world.

Content providers may identify themselves or participate anonymously. Content providers can also communicate with a wide audience by establishing a web site on which they can display text, graphics, or provide video, audio services and software. The ability to use these modes of communication to reach a potentially international audience is one of the most important aspects of the Internet. It has the potential to enhance social and political participation of individuals and enable the exchange of ideas across geographic and political boundaries. The Internet's capacity as an educational and cultural resource is enormous. Via the Internet users can access data bases, texts, journals, articles, reports, state documents, encyclopedias and legislation which are held by public and university libraries, government departments and organisations around the world. Many art galleries, museums and cultural institutions have also established web sites containing images and information about works in their collections, providing an enormous amount of musical, video and other audio material of educational value.

The Internet also enables researchers and students to communicate directly with others with similar interests around the world. For this reason the Internet has been an extremely important resource for a large number of educational organisations for over a decade and the use of on-line services is well-established in the university and research environments. In recent years, other sectors of education including schools have begun to utilise on-line technologies to extend the reach and effectiveness of teachers' work in terms of curriculum development, delivery of material and provision of professional support and development services.

The Internet also offers new possibilities for 'open learning' and learning by distance education. This has enormous potential to increase access to educational facilities for those in rural or non-metropolitan communities. It also enables students to enrol in a course of study with educational institutions around the globe. The Internet has the potential to become an important source of entertainment for users world wide. Already vast numbers of computer games, on-line magazines, newspapers, video and audio services are available on the Internet. Whilst many users can entertain themselves for hours 'surfing the net' for information, images and discussions regarding matters of interest to them, it is also important to note that in recent times many existing content industries are starting to use the Internet to deliver traditional audio and video products.

Although the bandwidth available in most countries currently precludes television broadcasts from easily being provided on-line, many predict that it is only a matter of time before full motion videos become widely available on the Internet. Over the next few years it is anticipated that the Internet will increasingly become a major source of the type of entertainment products which are currently available on television, radio, video and CD-ROM. As more secure methods of collecting payment for services over the Internet become available, it is expected that the Internet will also provide a common medium by which entertainment products are purchased. The international, interactive and decentralised nature of the Internet and its potential for making available vast quantities of content to and from anywhere in the world give rise to a number of legal and ethical challenges.

The following is not intended to be a complete discussion of all the issues which arise from the Internet, but an outline of some of those issues which create significant challenges, particularly in relation to content. Any individual who has access to the Internet can participate in the many modes of communication which function in the on-line environment, expressing their views in the form of text, images, or sound and accessing the vast array of content provided by others. For this reason the Internet has enormous potential to create a dynamic international on-line community in which the relative parity amongst users enhances freedom of speech and cultural, social, political, religious and linguistic diversity. However, it is important to recognise the critical role which access and active participation will play in this equation. Equitable access to the Internet remains a fundamental issue which will impact on the ability of individuals to participate in the benefits available through the Internet. This will be affected by the economic paradigms operating within both national and household frameworks.

The nature of the available telecommunications infrastructure and the costs of connecting to the network, typically via a service provider, will also impact on the opportunities presented to any given individual. Accordingly, ensuring equity of access to on-line services is emerging as a major challenge which is likely to have a concomitant impact on the issue of access to information, educational facilities and cultural resources and all of the opportunities which flow from these. It is also recognised that whilst the Internet provides the opportunity for immense diversity of content, at least at present, a significant proportion of Internet content appears to originate in Western liberal democracies, and particularly the United States. This material inevitably reflects some of the social, political and ethical values of those communities.

A substantial proportion of Internet content is also only available in the English language. One of the challenges if the Internet is to reach its potential as a diverse medium will be to ensure that it does not become an increasingly homogenised environment which enhances the dominance of particular languages and cultural perspectives. In this regard it is noted that many countries have adopted strategies for television and radio to ensure local content and community participation in those mediums. These strategies are not easily adopted or even appropriate for Internet communications. To maximise the diverse content and range of cultural and linguistic perspectives which can be accessed on-line it will be important to not only maximise access to the Internet but also to encourage all participants in the on-line environment to play an interactive role and contribute to the body of data which can be accessed by others through that medium. If content is provided from a wide variety of sources then the Internet may can maximise its enormous potential as a source of cultural, political, ethical and linguistic diversity which can increase understanding of cross-cultural issues and perceptions.

As many new and existing entertainment services, including video services, are delivered on-line in a manner which requires a more passive response from Internet users, it will be increasingly important to ensure that the Internet remains an interactive and participatory experience rather than become a predominantly passive medium. Most countries in the world place some restrictions on the type of material which may be possessed and/or disseminated within their borders. The extent and degree to which material in any given country is subject to restrictions reflects its particular political, cultural, religious and legal traditions. These traditions vary immensely around the world.

Even where there is some consistency across jurisdictions relating to certain material, such as child pornography, the specific provisions of the various laws relating to the topic can differ significantly, making prosecution and international cooperation difficult. Even determining what is illegal in any particular country can be difficult due to the generality of the various national laws. For example, laws often set out broad categories of restricted material, such as 'obscene' material, and rely on the discretion of courts to give content to the prohibition. This makes it particularly difficult to identify what is prohibited in any given country at any given time. The ability to communicate anonymously in the on-line environment, which enables users to express themselves in a manner that may not be possible in the off-line world, also renders detection of those providing and accessing material which is prohibited extremely difficult.

Anonymous re-mailing services can exacerbate this difficulty as Internet messages can be re-routed and copied in such a way that it is not possible to reliably ascertain their source. The encryption of content adds a further dimension to the difficulties of dealing with illegal material in the on-line environment. Whilst certain kinds of content may be appropriate for adults to access, it may be unsuitable for children. Material which is sexually explicit or violent is often included in the type of content which is considered unsuitable or harmful for minors. Perceptions about the types of material which are suitable for children and young people vary immensely not only across national boundaries but also across cultures, religions and political systems. In some communities there is a high level of concern regarding sex and nudity, while in others material containing violent matter or drug abuse is considered to be the most offensive. Even within fairly homogeneous cultures there may be a wide range of differing views held about the appropriateness of certain material for minors, particularly where the material relates to sex, nudity, violence, language, and drug use. In existing media many mechanisms have been adopted to minimise children's access to unsuitable material. These range from age restrictions on material which can be purchased or screened in cinemas to time zone classifications which restrict the type of programs which can be screened on television at times when children are likely to be watching. However, the availability of material which is considered unsuitable or harmful for minors presents particular challenges in the context of the Internet.

The Internet allows material to be accessed at any time in an interactive manner. Most material is not restricted in any way, the main exception being material which requires credit card details or some other form of payment is required. Accordingly, there is growing concern about the ability of minors to access material which is unsuitable for them but at the same time a recognition of the rights of adults to provide and access material which is legal in the off-line world. In response to this concern a number of technical options, including filter software products and the Platform for Internet Content Selection (PICS) have been developed. One of the important challenges in this area will be to ensure that these products are able to accommodate the diverse range of views and cultural perspectives which prevail around the world in relation to the protection of minors. The international and decentralised nature of the Internet gives rise to a vast range of issues which challenge the mechanism previously used to deal with these matters on a domestic basis. The issues raised in the on-line environment include privacy, intellectual property, defamation, issues of electronic commerce and consumer protection, taxation and on-line gambling, along with illegal content and content which may be harmful to minors, to name a few.

The role and responsibilities which service providers can and should have in relation to these matters is an area in respect of which there has been widespread debate and raises many technical, legal and philosophical issues. Part of the difficulty stems from the complex nature of the service providers role in relation to providing, disseminating and enabling access to content. In some situations service providers seek to exercise some control over the content that is available through their service whilst in others they may have no knowledge or ability to control the content which is provided or accessed by users or content providers. In such an environment it is extremely difficult to allocate legal responsibility in same the manner that may have been possible in traditional broadcasting and publication models, creating many legal and ethical uncertainties. The Internet presents immense legal and ethical challenges, particularly in relation to content. It must be accepted that by its very nature the Internet cannot be controlled by any central body and that its dynamic nature means that it is impossible to even assess the amount or nature of Internet content at any given time.

Most countries have some laws which makes it an offence to publish and/or distribute certain material. In some countries it is also an offence to possess certain material, such as child pornography. In some cases existing legislation regarding the publication, distribution and possession of certain types of content has been drafted in a manner which enables it to encompass material transmitted and accessed on-line. However, in other jurisdictions specific legislation to deal with illegal content in the on-line environment has been proposed or introduced. In Singapore licensees are required to use their best efforts to ensure that their services does not include Internet content which is 'against the public interest, public order, national harmony or which offends against good taste or decency'. The scheme identifies particular Internet content which falls within this category. This includes, inter alia, content "which propagate permissiveness or promiscuity", "tends to bring the Government of Singapore into hatred or contempt, or which excites disaffection against the Government of Singapore." In contrast it seems that at least some content of this nature would not be illegal in the United Kingdom and Australia. In the United Kingdom codes of practice are being utilised to place obligations on service providers to deal with, and where possible, remove illegal content from their servers once it has been identified. In exchange for complying with these procedures service providers may receive some protection from prosecution . In Australia the proposed regulatory regime also envisages that codes of practice for service providers will include appropriate procedures to deal with illegal content if and when it has been brought to a service providers attention. It has been suggested that compliance with codes of practice could be a defence in any prosecution against a service provider.

One of the recent responses to the issue of illegal content has been the setting up of reporting agencies, often referred to as 'e-mail hotlines'. These agencies enable Internet users who locate content which they believe is illegal to report their finding to a reporting agency which will investigate the content and may take action in relation to the material. To date e-mail hotline services have been identified in Singapore and the United Kingdom. In the United Kingdom an e-mail hotline has been set up under the Safety-Net Initiative. The Hotline service is operated by Internet Watch and "aims to enhance the enormous potential of the Internet to inform, educate, entertain and conduct business by ... hindering the use of the Internet to transmit material which is illegal in the UK". The first priority of the scheme is child pornography.

Internet Watch operates by encouraging Internet users to report content which they believe to be child pornography. Reports can be made by telephone, facsimile or e-mail and should contain a brief description of the material in question and the location of the site (i.e the world wide web address or the Usenet newsgroup details). Where the material has been identified as being sourced within the United Kingdom then Internet Watch will request that the relevant service provider contact the person who has placed the material on-line and seek to have the material removed. If material is not removed and/or if it involves child pornography, then Internet Watch will forward details to the Police.

Under the scheme the police are to provide feedback to Internet Watch on the outcome of their report. Where the material is sourced from outside of the United Kingdom then Internet Watch will forward to the police the information about the site who will notify the relevant overseas law enforcement agency. In Singapore, as part of its regulatory regime established in July 1996, the Singapore Broadcasting Authority has also set up a 'hotline' for identifying 'objectionable content'. The SBA has stated that the success of Internet content will depend very much on industry self-regulation and community action and has welcomed public assistance in the identification of material which is considered 'objectionable' under the laws of Singapore. Reports can be made by e-mail, telephone or post. In Australia the Australian Broadcasting Authority in its Report on the Content of On-Line Services supported in principle the establishment of e-mail hotlines for the reporting of child pornography. The ABA understands that the police bodies and law enforcement bodies are presently examining the viability of establishing such an agency in Australia.

Parental or teacher supervision is the most effective way of managing children's access to the Internet. However, it is widely recognised that this is not always possible and over the last decade, a range of software products have been developed for use on computers in the home and in schools in response to the perceived need for parents, teachers and supervisors to filter out or block Internet content which they do not consider suitable for minors in their care. Filter software can be provided to the user by the on-line service provider or purchased independently by the consumer for use at the individual computer level. Some service providers also offer a filtering service which is specifically designed for use by minors. Filtering programs work in three main ways:

1. sites are blocked with reference to a list of known newsgroups, world wide web sites, File Transfer Protocol (FTP) and Gopher sites. Censoring decisions may be made centrally by the software producer with sites updated regularly, and/or by users instructing their system to block a particular site(s);

2. requests for, or receipt of, information which contains specified keywords or phrases are blocked. The keywords or phrases can be specified by the software manufacturer or by the end users who can manage the blocking of web sites by entering keywords and phrases in accordance with criteria they consider appropriate; and

3. all sites are blocked except those which are specified by the supervisor ('blanket blocking'). These programs usually provide an original unblocked list of known educational sites, and the supervisor is able to unblock new sites through a password secured interface.

Some products enable parents to combine some of these functions, while others offer additional features such as auditing of all on-line activity, including listing sites accessed, restricting the amount of time spent on-line and limiting access to some services such as bulletin boards. Whilst the first generation of filter products offer parents some tools to control their children's access to unsuitable material, some users have found that they have a number of limitations. For example, products which are based on recognition of keywords and phrases are not able to filter explicit graphic images or deal with encrypted data or transposed text. Conversely, sites of value to the user may also be blocked if they contain specified keywords or phrases. For example, press reports stated that at one time access to the White House web site was blocked by a filter responding to the word 'couple'. Where software producers are responsible for the blocking of material they may restrict content which is considered acceptable to the parent/supervisor.

Where filter software operates by means of 'blanket' blocking, access to a considerable amount of potentially valuable material would be denied and parents and teachers would in many cases have to allocate considerable resources to enable access to appropriate material. However, there have been some recent international developments with content and selection software which have provided additional options for parents. This technology is called the Platform for Internet Content Selection (PICS). PICS was developed by the World Wide Web Consortium (W3C). W3C is a non-governmental cross-industry group which has offices in USA, France and Japan and comprises representatives of the computer, communications and content industries, as well as trade associations and public interest groups. PICS works by establishing a series of file formats that allows independent rating services to label Internet content in a form that can be recognised by PICS enabled software. The PICS labelling conventions do not dictate the use of any particular labelling scheme or determine who should pay attention to which labels. The PICS technology allows any organisation or individual to develop a labelling system which reflects their tastes and standards and, if they wish, enable others to also use these labels.

PICS compatible software can be set to block out all unrated content, or to only block content which has been rated in a certain manner. There are a number of scenarios in which PICS labels can be used. For example, labels may be developed to indicate whether Internet content contains sexual or violent material, enabling parents to select or block the material accordingly. A teacher might label a set of materials which are relevant to an astronomy lesson and block student access to everything else during that class. Those concerned about Nazi propaganda and other hate-speech available on-line, could label material that is historically inaccurate or that promotes hate, and businesses may wish to use labels to block their employees from visiting recreational sites during hours of office hours.

Labelling can be applied directly by content providers at the time or after a site is posted on the Internet or it can be applied by a third party in accordance with an established labelling system. The creators of PICS envisaged that it could be used to support a large number of different labelling schemes which may have a multitude of different purposes. A number of organisations have already begun to establish labelling schemes which can interact with the PICS standards, most of which have been developed in North America and aim to assist parents in managing their children's access to Internet content. Examples are the Recreational Software Advisory Council labelling scheme for the Internet (RSACi), SafeSurf, Cyber Patrol and Net Shepherd. One of the PICS compatible labelling schemes which has gained increasing prominence is the descriptive labelling scheme developed by the Recreational Software Advisory Council (RSAC) and is discussed below by way of example. The RSACi labelling system addresses four matters. These are the level of violence, sex, nudity, and language, including hate language, which a site contains. Internet content can be given a rating between 0 and 4 on each of these topics.

The label aims to provide a description of the content in an Internet site rather than make a judgement about the appropriateness of content for any given audience or purpose. In some ways the descriptive RSAC labels can be seen as analogous to the labels applied to foodstuffs which merely provide information about ingredients of a product, rather than vouch for its suitability for consumption. One of the uses of a descriptive labelling schemes is that it enables parents to set their own standards about the material which they or their children access. For example, parents who are concerned about sexual content are able to set their PICS compatible software to block out material which has been given a high rating for sexual content. Other parents may be more concerned about language and/or violence and so can also can set their software to block out highly rated material of this nature. If the material has been rated then parents can use the labels to control Internet content, regardless of where they or the content is located. Importantly, those who are not concerned to block their own access to Internet materials need not activate those tools. A proliferation of PICS compatible labelling schemes, perhaps being developed by a range of industry, community and governmental bodies around the world could serve many functions, including giving consumers a range of choices in relation to the values and perspectives which underpin the various labelling schemes and the purposes for which they can be used. This has the ability to reflect a diversity of different cultures and values and provide individuals with real choices about the filtering software and nature of Internet content which they access. However, for labels to be a truly effective tool for parents and supervisors many argue that a critical mass of content needs to be labelled. This raises the issue of whether it would be advantageous to develop a small number of international labelling schemes which can be widely recognised by content providers and users around the globe.

The Safety-Net initiative developed in the United Kingdom originally supported the use of the RSACi labeling scheme and proposed that service providers require their users to rate their web sites using RSACi labels. However, the ABA understands that there have been some recent developments in this regard and that Internet Watch Foundation has undertaken to work with the on-line industry in that country to develop a PICS compatible labeling scheme which meets the specific requirements of users in the United Kingdom.

The impacts of Globalization, Relativism, the New World Order, Materialism, Egocentricism, Hyper Consumerism, invasive technologies, the uncontrollable flood of information, the advent of genetic manipulation and perhaps genetic control, the corrosion of the notion of the sacred in modern post-industrial societies and many other factors have disturbed the ladder of values in each and every society. The insatiable greed for more instant pleasure has added a spinning potential to the tempo of change. Due to this uncontrollable hyper acceleration in all the venues of life including cyber crime, some would state that a rational utilitarian scale of values could govern human behaviour. To prevent the loss of hundreds of thousands of dollars in wasted man-hours and bandwidth more and more employers are using special software to monitor their employees' Web browsing and e-mail traffic".

Marketers can spy on you by using cookies. A cookie is a unique text file that is placed on your hard drive the first time you access certain websites. It is like a personal serial number used to identify your computer on your next visit to the site but the cookie also enables the marketers to gather information about your browsing preferences. According to the Washington based privacy research group EPIC, 86 out of 100 tested online companies work with cookies. The gathered information about the customers could be sold to other persons or entities".Hackers can spy on you by using Trojan horses coming in the guise of backdoor computer programs which once infiltrating into your computer allows hackers to access it and take control. Hackers can even spy on your E-mail as it passes through the several web servers. At any of these relay points your message is vulnerable to snooping.

Skillful hackers can also hijack a router and then read or mess around with the text messages stored in it. Sniffer programs may scan traffic for specified terms, cyber snoops can capture Internet account login IDS & passwords and use them to surf the web at owner's expense and web based E-mail services are particularly open to intruders. Some sovereign states run electronic surveillance systems around the world and scan the web for signs of criminal activity, monitoring E-mail communications eavesdropping on chat room conversations and generally tracking the traffic on the net. Echelon, a massive cold war-era surveillance network run by the intelligence services of the U.S., U.K., Canada New Zealand and Australia, is the world's most extensive spy system for nonmilitary targets and the one most likely to be watching as you roam the Web. Some 90% of Net traffic is said to be scanned by Echelon. Several countries also run their own national Web surveillance systems.

According to Duncan Campbell "the Echelon system can access and process all of the world's satellite communications automatically". A large part of Echelon is devoted to the INTELSAT network of Geo stationary communications satellites. Cable tapping is harder, however, as with cryptography itself Echelon is fighting a loosing battle. As more and more phones become low power digital devices, the range over which they can be monitored and the effort needed to decode them increases, a brand new wireless technology called pulse wireless - already used by the security services - promises to make many transmission virtually undetectable. By autumn of this year, the Echelon interception system will be subject to a legal battle that threatens to blow the lid on this covert surveillance network Echelon when the issue reaches the courts.

David Nataf of the Jean Pierre Millet law firm in Paris is leading the assault on America's National Security Agency (NSA). The plaintiffs, several French corporations and individuals who cannot be identified, allege that the (NSA) has spied on them illegally. He says his team has enough evidence against the (NSA) to pursue damages for lost business and for illegal covert activity. At the center of the allegations is evidence implicating the (NSA's) involvement in spying on European nations' commercial dealings. Nataf's team will try to convince the American courts that stolen information was passed onto US companies, giving them an unfair advantage over their French competitors. In March 2000, a former CIA director, James Woolsey, confirmed that the US monitors European communications to keep an eye on any economic bribery activities.

A Scientific and Technical Options Assessment (STOA) report called Development of Surveillance Technology and Risk of Abuse of Economic Information presented to the European Union December 1999 concludes that: 'Although it is very difficult to quantify the losses caused by industrial espionage, the losses incurred by European firms can reasonably be put at several billion Euros per year'. These are some of the issues affecting the Right of Privacy on the networks. The matrix of interceptors includes individuals, corporations, multinational companies and even sovereign states. Efforts are evolving to inquire into these interception activities and even to condone their acts pursuant to the right of privacy on the networks and global communication. As with any issue involving communities at large, a multitude of interception techniques have been described and elaborated on. Some even sound extremely credible and others are generally discarded as unimaginable at the current state of technology.

The law has a functional role by deterring any potential perpetrator from committing a criminal act and it also has a curative effect in devolving compensations for damages if an illicit act is committed. The legal texts covering this area are various as we have previously mentioned and they constitute two faces of one coin. One face is information protection laws and the other is telecommunications protection laws. Their symbiotic effect produces the legal deterrent and protection. To be criminalized and penalized by the law, the acts of violation of the right of privacy should constitute crimes in conformity with the old Latin rule. We should bear in mind that criminal law texts are interpreted very strictly.

Virtual Forum on INFOethics

VF-INFOethics is an open worldwide electronic discussion forum carried out from October 1997 to April 1998. This forum was organized as a follow-up to a recommendation made by the participants at the first INFOethics Congress held in Monaco from 10 to 12 March 1997. The forum was designed and managed by the Information Science Department of the University of Konstanz. VF-INFOethics is not a substitute for meetings in a real-life environment — the advantage of face-to-face communication is too obvious and knowledge and experience with electronic forums is not yet wide-spread enough, at least not among UNESCO experts, who are normally not the typical Internet users. But experimenting with electronic forums can provide UNESCO with knowledge about the potentials of the new medium and can contribute to a more extended word-wide awareness about the importance of information ethics in a globalizing information society. VF-INFOethics thus supports UNESCO's objective as a world-wide laboratory of ideas, in this case via a forum on information ethics, identifying ethical principles, guiding action, devising immaterial strategies and mobilizing political leaders in their resolve to implement them. As potentials or value-added effects of electronic communication forums the following deserve mention:

- Electronic communication forums allow exchange of information between people who are not likely to meet in real life.

- Electronic communication forums, organized according to hypertext principles, allow flexible navigation in heterogeneous information material and can thus develop into a platform of knowledge with respect to the topic of the forum.

- Electronic communication forums, in a Web-based technical environment are normally organized in an asynchronous mode (although synchronous chat techniques or tele-conferencing facilities are becoming more and more available for forum purposes as well). Asynchronous communication allows quasi real-time reactions to the forum's statements but also allows delayed reactions after a period of information gathering or, simply, of thinking.

- Electronic communication forums, compared with the high costs for real conferences with participants from all over the world, are a cheap technology once the technical equipment is available.

- Electronic communication forums, in particular when data-base supported, allow flexible adaptation to different users' needs/expectations, or to users' dialogue behaviour, and to different pre-established parameters such as access and editing rights.

The hopes for VF-INFOethics were only moderately high because we could not expect that knowledge and experience with new electronic communication devices would be very advanced among UNESCO experts. This was all the more likely, given the fact that we tried to avoid an Anglo-saxon and Western-Europe dominated expertise and insisted instead on selecting people from all over the world. The particants were chosen on the basis of UNESCO expertise and recommendations from active members. Only these experts, altogether about 60, had the right to write, but the forum, as a WWW application, was open to the public for reading purposes. The forum's main objective was to augment knowledge and public awareness on topics concerning information ethics and to provide UNESCO with recommendations for further action in the field of information ethics based on the world-wide electronic discussion among experts in the field. In addition to statements from experts, additional information, for example references to pertinent literature on information ethics, to other web sites, to data bases, and to other discussion groups with a similar scope was provided by the central Constance monitoring group of VF-INFOethics. Additional links could be provided by all members of VF-INFOethics. VF-INFOethics has thus developed into an open forum, a platform, or a market place with numerous links to the world's knowledge on information ethics. The INFOethics forum was carried out in two rounds. The first round lasted from October 97 until the end of the year 1998. The second round was opened for discussion as of Februar 20th 1998.

At the end of round 2, UNESCO can be provided with recommendations for further action. It is very likely that the forum will continue to be an electronic floor for UNESCO-related discussions on INFOethics and will then be opened to a broader UNESCO public or to the public in general. This, of course, will raise many new problems. In the near future, the forum will be used before, during and after the second UNESCO conference on INFOethics, which will take place in October 1998, again in Monte Carlo. The software, which was developed for VF-INFOethics and which is continously being improved, can be used for other UNESCO activities, in particular by national commissions for UNESCO or for educational purposes. At the moment, we are using the VF-INFOethics software for a virtually organized course on information ethics in the information science curriculum at the University of Konstanz, Germany. The forum was opened with a brief general statement about the concept of information ethics:

Information ethics, in general, is the study of commonly held values related to the belief in equality of access, justice and mutual respect arising from the development and application of new information and telecommunications technologies (e.g. the Internet). Information ethics concerns many fields such as philosophy (ethics), anthropology/ethnology, linguistics, economics, law, sociology, political science, education, religion/theology, artificial intelligence, information and computer science. Information ethics covers both the private/individual and the public/institutional aspects of ethical problems, more and more on a global basis. For many people, information ethics is likely to be considered as a substitute for traditional civic behavior in the advancing global information society. For UNESCO, information ethics is particularly related to science, education, culture, and civil society in general, both in developed and in developing countries.

The following questions were formulated with respect to the role of UNESCO on the topic ,Information rich and information poor': What can UNESCO do to prevent modern societies from being divided into the information elite and the information underprivileged? Is there a need and a chance for UNESCO to fill the widening "abstraction gap" between the dominant information rich and the information poor? Is UNESCO an appropriate advocate to defend the rights of the information underprivileged? What is the role of organizations such as UNESCO in overcoming the information and communication gap both within countries and between them?

'Information as a public and/or a private good' stimulated some discussion about the status of information in modern societies. Some concern was expressed about the negative effects of modern information structures (virtualization) on the job market. The participants did not see any realistic alternative economic model by which the shortcomings of the neo-liberalism approach could be overcome. It was suggested that cooperatives may play a major role in the usage of information as a common good. UNESCO should not get involved in general abstract discussions about a new world order. Instead UNESCO should concentrate on feasible projects such as supporting efforts for the digitization of public information (as the world people's heritage) as a counterweight to the power of the market, where information is considered a commodity only. The role of copyright should be reconsidered as well in order to define a new generally accepted fair use of information. By encouraging free access to the world's public knowledge (the people's own heritage) UNESCO can contribute to establishing a counterweight to the power of the market, where information is considered a commodity to be paid for.

UNESCO should use a set amount of funds to support the digitization of public material (e.g. to finance portable scanners). The role of copyright (so far mainly used to enforce market rights) should be reconsidered. Particularly, the rights of users to access public materials should be balanced against the predominantly private exploitation of information. Preservation and transmission of information was considered as among the ethical responsibilities of the present for future generations. The following questions were formulated with respect to the role of UNESCO on the topic ‚Trust, ownership, and validity of information in cyberspace':

What can be done by UNESCO in order to establish an ethics instrument for information/content providers by which they may be obliged to care for trustworthy, approved, or true information? Which is the main role of UNESCO in the new property right debate, for example on digital objects? What can UNESCO do to establish a new "fair use" and/or "copyleft" of information which establishes a compromise between the rights of the holders and the interests of society to have free access to information? Can UNESCO play an active role in establishing trust in information services and electronic markets, in particular when sensitive subjects are involved, such as medicine, law, or political information? Is UNESCO an appropriate and world-wide accepted institution to develop, maintain, and survey generally accepted quality criteria for the reliability and authenticity of information services? What is the role of UNESCO in establishing trust in machine intelligence and services such as intelligent agents or in keeping it under public control?

There was an innovative and provocative proposal to rethink the role of copyright: It doesn't make any sense for authors who already get paid by public institutions to receive additional copyright income. Giving up copyright income could break the circle of high prices and lack of access, at least in scientific environments. Access to the world's knowledge should have higher priority than supporting commercial interest in information commodities. A different answer may be required with respect to entertainment and literature. On the other hand it was not considered realistic that authors would voluntarily give up commercial rights. Therefore it is not sufficient to change our attitude towards ownership and profit.

A solution could be for publishing companies to pay a certain percentage of the author's income to the public, which is explicitly designed for supporting the construction of a powerful and royalty-free world wide public domain of information. This idea of sharing profits from knowledge products can be extended to all organizations which produce value-adding information/ knowledge products originally based on publicly produced and financed primary/raw information for the market. UNESCO is not either WIPO or WTO (although the protection of authors/publishers' rights cannot be ignored, it is not the main concern for UNESCO). Instead UNESCO must bring its own added value to the debate on intellectual property rights, and this means to promote the free flow of ideas by word and image, to give fresh impulse to popular education, and to support all means for the diffusion of knowledge.

All scientific articles produced by public universities or public laboratories could be made freely available on the servers of these institutions. UNESCO should take the lead in a world wide movement to promote this public domain information, and present innovative ideas to ensure distribution and free access to it. In particular with respect to developing countries, economic barriers created by a purely market oriented approach towards knowledge and information need to be overcome. UNESCO should use all its prestige to convince governments and institutions involved in the information/knowledge industry all over the world that they should share profits from knowledge products (especially those which are originally based on publicly produced and financed primary/raw information) with public institutions. These institutions then can produce value-added free-access information for those who cannot afford to pay for it.

Although the concept of information ethics was a topic of discussion in itself and was permanently referredto, there was no formal agreement about this concept besides general remarks such as that information ethics deals with principles of equality, justice and mutual respect under the conditions of a global information society. Global networks and electronic market places and information services (in the Internet and other prorietary networks) are the environment and the only means in which and through which information ethics develops. One can doubt whether there is a need (or a possibility) for something like information ethics (or science ethics or market ethics) in addition to ethics in general.

The principles of ethics in general — if any — would also be valid for information ethics in particular. The forum's participants were particularly careful in simply transferring western ideas to a global information world and were also very concerned that the unification influence of the global Internet can lead to an unwanted dominant general and ethical culture. This is clearly to be seen on (ethical) topics such as property right, violence in the media, information access and information equity, individual freedom of information, where Western philosophical, political, and economic traditions dominate. Information ethics is not a matter of abstract academic (philosophical) discussion and cannot result in a new (single) world order of information behaviour, but can be a permanent world-wide process of exchange of positions between people who are involved in structuring the new information world.

The global information society is thus a platform for information ethics and the result of the discussion cannot be a single world information ethics but the development of an ethos that makes the public aware and sensitive of the need to take a responsible and not only merely economically determined approach towards information, its production, distribution and usage. This is the major information ethic topic in the information society. The topic is in its global character comparable to ecological questions and should thus be treated on the same level of political decision-making and public disussion. There is a real need for an international information agenda. What VF-INFOethics thus recommends is the development of a world-wide public responsibilty for information equity (an information ethos) by establishing an institutionalized dialog on information policy issues at a world level, 'some authors hold that a new UN/UNESCO information agency would be an approriate institutional means—and by supporting an open world forum (or many interlinked forums) on information ethics, using the electronic medium and other media as well.

Both an institutionalized and a communicative approach will create global (and local!) information policies and information cultures. This means that one should give up the ideal of a rational, clean and transparent ethical world information order, and see the multi-cultural reality not as a threat but as an opportunity. The continuing globalization of all aspects of the production, distribution and usage of information is the central challenge for information ethics.

The production of information is based on the need for information and refers to its content and quality. The distribution of information raises the question of information ownership and depends on the information resources in which information is represented and on the design and management of information market places where information can be accessed and exchanged. The usage of information is mainly a question of competence and money — being informationally educated in order to profit from the information resources and being able to pay for the costs of information usage. This is a (political) question of information equity or inequity or how to overcome information gaps. Considering the importance of the global information society, it has turned out that the participants were mainly concerned about the growing gap between those who are able and willing to take advantage of modern information and communication technology and those who are not.

The problem of information gaps cannot be restricted to the difference between developed and developing countries but is a problem in all societies, whatever their technological status. If access to information and the possibility to actively take part in the exchange of knowledge (to have the right to read and write in open information environments) is the necessary basis for all activities in our public and private life, then it is UNESCO's responsibility to support all activities which aim at establishing an information balance in the information society. A society is information-balanced when information gaps can be overcome.

Therefore a consideration of information equity seems to be at the center of all ethical discussion. This is not a technological problem. It cannot be solved by providing everyone in the world with a computer and telecommunication equipment (although the importance of such a programme — to provide in principle everyone with the technological basis needed — should not be underestimated), but by solving the information problem.

2

Emergence of Internet

Price and quality differentiation are valuable tools that can provide higher revenues and increase utilization efficiency of a network, and thus in general increase social welfare. Such measures, most noticeable in airline pricing, are spreading to many services and products, especially high-tech ones. However, it appears that as communication services become less expensive and are used more frequently, those arguments lose out to customers' desire for simplicity. In practice, user preferences express themselves through willingness to pay more for simple pricing plans.

In addition, there is a strong "threshhold" effect to usage-sensitive billing. Even tiny charges based on utilization decrease usage substantially. In a rapidly growing market, it is in the service providers' interest to encourage usage, and that argues for simple, preferably flat rate, pricing.

Historical evidence suggests that when service costs decrease, such arguments prevail over the need to operate a network at high utilization levels and to extract the highest possible revenues. Communication services have long exhibited many characteristics of modern high-tech industries, namely high fixed costs, network effects, and difficulty in allocating costs among many products and services.

When prices are high, and purchases infrequent, airline-style "yield management" is likely to dominate. On the other hand, when prices are low, and a service is used many times a day, simple pricing and uniformly high quality are likely to be more common.

Historical analogies as well as current expenditure data also suggest that in the "digital convergence" of broadcasting and point-to-point communications, it is the latter that will dominate in shaping the evolution of the Internet. The current preoccupation with professionally produced "content" is probably more a distraction than help in planning for the future.

The development of the Internet is likely to be determined by the same growth of the myriad unpredictable commercial and social interactions that have fueled other communication services. The Internet has historically treated all packets equally, and pricing has been predominantly through flat monthly rates depending only on the size of access links, not on usage.

Today, there is a strong momentum towards changing both of these principles. Although flat-rate continues to be the predominant form in which Internet access is sold, that form of pricing is unviable. Flat-rate pricing encourages waste and requires 20 percent of users who account for 80 percent of the traffic to be subsidized by other users and other forms of revenue.

Furthermore, flat-rate pricing is incompatible with quality-differentiated services. There is extensive work on development of multiple service levels, typically with some implied guarantee of performance, usually referred to as Quality of Service (QoS). If those are deployed, they will necessarily require pricing schemes more complicated than the standard flat rate ones. The driving force behind these developments is economic, based on the view that it is not feasible to provide satisfactory levels of quality for all transmissions at a reasonable cost.

There is also concern (expressed in the quote above) about fairness of light users subsidizing heavy ones under the current scheme. While the momentum is towards introduction of QoS and more complicated pricing systems, there have always been voices arguing in favour of preserving the simplicity of both operations and pricing of the current Internet. Their counterarguments can be substantiated through evaluations of the costs of multiple service levels to end users, and on considerations of what utility users derive from data networks.

Shortage of bandwidth is less of a problem than is often thought, and the general complexity of the system is a large barrier. An important observation behind many of the arguments in those papers is that what users really care about are fast transactions. As a result, whenever they can afford it, they run their links at low utilizations, since the main benefit they derive comes from the ability to burst at high speeds for short periods.

In such an environment, flat rate pricing is most appropriate, and QoS does not help much. However unsound it may have seemed, unlimited local calling for a flat monthly fee for residential users has persisted in most of the United States for all of the 20th century. It seems worth exploring why it did, what effects that has had in comparison with other countries that adopted usage-sensitive pricing, why it is being reintroduced in many of those countries, and what conclusions we can draw from this about the likely future of the Internet.

History never repeats exactly, but there are frequent recurring themes that illuminate the present and hopefully can help make better choices for the future. While QoS and sophisticated pricing schemes are widely regarded as necessary for the future of the Internet, the trend in other communication services has almost uniformly been in the opposite direction.

In long distance voice telephony, the most popular plans are the simple ones that are independent of time of day or distance. Even in the Internet arena, the trend so far has been largely towards simple flat rates. A decade ago, the mass market online services, such as CompuServe, Prodigy, and AOL charged not just for minutes of connect time, but even for individual email messages.

Email charges were eliminated first. By the middle 1990s, these services were also forced by subscriber complaints and competition from other ISPs to switch to unlimited access for a flat monthly fee. Although simplicity in pricing has been the general trend, it is important to recognize that there is persuasive logic to differentiated services.

Even in the absence of quality differentiations, there are good reasons for pricing according to usage, as is done with electricity. Some of the arguments in this direction will be reviewed later. A major problem with such measures, though, is that usage sensitive charging, even with very low rates, lowers usage, often dramatically. Sometimes that is desirable.

Western Europe is beginning to reintroduce forms of flat rate local phone calling precisely in order to stimulate Internet usage, which lags behind that in North America. Numerous examples are presented later to show that the best way to stimulate usage is to have flat rates.

The Internet is expected to continue growing and to penetrate ever more deeply into our lives. Hence the competition among ISPs will be won by those who can entice their subscribers to make the fullest use of the services that are offered. Flat rates or approximations to them are among the most powerful tools in this competition. The general trend has been for each communication service to offer higher quality and lower prices. This has gone hand in hand with higher usage, and higher total revenues.

A particularly telling instance of the trend towards simplification in communication is the tendency for prices to become distance-insensitive as a service evolves. The basic justification for the development of quality-differentiated service levels on the Internet is the perception that transmission and switching resources are expensive, and therefore high quality cannot be provided uniformly for all traffic. Yet that does not seem to have been a barrier for other communication services.

The distance dependence in pricing of mail, telegraph, telephone, and even data network services has historically decreased, or even disappeared completely. Long distance transmission is regarded as more valuable. Thus the decrease in distance dependence of pricing provides an even stronger argument than that of the hypothetical Martian.

Perhaps an even more interesting point of view goes even deeper into an analysis of possible forms of pricing. A schedule of charges based simply on distance is already a major concession to the desire for simplicity, and away from optimality in either revenue extraction or in relating prices to costs.

A sounder procedure is to investigate more carefully what factors contributed to historical developments, and what influence they might have in the future. There are, after all, reasonable arguments against simplicity. Sophisticated strategies for quality differentiation and price discrimination are common. They are perhaps most noticeable in airline yield management, but are spreading to other areas.

While there are sound arguments for quality differentiation and price discrimination, there are also economic arguments against them, based on economic models that favour bundling. Perhaps more important, such practices conflict with the strong preference that people have for simple pricing, especially for flat rate schemes.

There are many reasons for this preference. The insurance aspect is important. On the other hand, the search for optimal efficiency has usually been abandoned in favour of simplicity for small and frequent transactions. The long history illustrates how the decreasing prices of communication services, the fruit of improving technology and of economies of scale, have gone hand in hand with the trend towards greater simplicity. It seems reasonable to expect that a similar division between the quest for optimal efficiency on one hand, and simplicity on the other, will hold in the future. It will be easier for service providers to implement complicated pricing schemes.

There will also be more tools helping consumers to navigate the maze of choices. However, both factors have been operating for a long time and that appears only to have strengthened people's desire for simplicity. The Internet is leading to an unprecedented proliferation of choices in goods and services, straining human capacity to deal with all the complexities.

Therefore the balance between optimization and simplicity is likely to remain where it has been, in spite of the developments in technology. That is a major reason that airline tickets are much more likely to be sold through complicated schemes than voice calls.

Even in the U.S., which is affluent, and has a large air transport industry, there is only about one round trip per person per year by air, at a cost of around $400. Thus airplane tickets are expensive and are bought relatively infrequently. Further, air transport is a mature industry, and costs are declining slowly. On the other hand, on average each U.S. inhabitant is engaged in about a dozen phone calls per day, each typically lasting about three minutes, and costing either nothing or a fraction of a dollar.

Human attention may be the ultimate scarce resource. The historical trend of increasing volumes and decreasing costs in communications is illustrated by comparing the purchase of a book today to the receipt of a letter in England in the the early 19th century. In 1834, about 5 letters were mailed per person per year in England.

In most parts of the country, the recipient had to learn that a letter was waiting, go to the post office and pay a fee that averaged what about two hours of work cost. In contrast, in the U.S. of 1994, there were about two pieces of mail delivered per person per day. The cost of each piece was under two minutes' wages for an average worker.

Today, half a dozen years later, we are in the in the Amazon.com era. Those additional non-monetary book purchase costs can be decreased, as we can order books with a few keystrokes and mouse clicks, and have them delivered to our house a day or two later. Thus in terms of relative costs, books today are acquired more often and cost less than letters 170 years ago.

Currently there are widespread expectations that "content," usually denoting professionally produced multimedia traffic, will dominate the Internet. However, even if the volume of multimedia traffic does exceed that of other transmissions, designing the network primarily for such traffic is likely to be a mistake.

Historical evidence, including current statistics, shows that people are willing to spend far more on point-to-point communication than on entertainment. Thus it is unlikely that professionally produced multimedia traffic will determine the evolution of the Internet. For example, in the early 19th century, U.S. postal policy was preoccupied with broadcast-type communication, namely through newspapers. Distribution of newspapers was subsidized to an extraordinary degree by regular letters, which brought in most of the money. Eventually public pressure forced policy makers to lower the prices of letters, which led to an upsurge of traffic.

Historical analogies are interesting, but may not always apply to a new technologies. Perhaps most important, prices have been increasing in recent years for most of the Internet. This is a seldom-noted phenomenon that is almost unique among modern high-tech industries in which demand has been increasing and technological progress has been stunningly fast.

It is likely that this increase in transmission prices has been responsible for much of the demand for QoS and complicated pricing. Once prices start plummeting overall, as they have begun to do on some routes, it seems likely that providing more bandwidth will be seen to be more attractive than forcing complicated schemes on users. There are two other ways in which the Internet is often claimed to differ from other communication services.

One is in the possibility for a "tragedy of the commons," in which flat rate pricing leads users to saturate any links that are offered. The other is in the independence of traffic from distance. Service providers would act as insurance companies, using prior usage, demographics, and other information to fashion customized bundled offers that would meet the demands for simplicity and flexibility.

Most standard works, such as, concentrate on optimizing some conventional quantitative utility function, and treat customer desires as irrelevant, or else as irrational annoyances that interfere with clever and efficient schemes.

It presents extensive historical and current data about customer preferences, explores the reasons for such preferences, and considers the effects of catering to them.

It argues that however irrational such preferences may seem, they should be paid attention to. It shows that, generally, such a course of action is likely to be best for rapidly growing communication services like the Internet.

Technology is boosting the capacity of all networks. Therefore customers have to be encouraged to increase usage, to fill this growing capacity. Carriers that fail to persuade their customers to move on to higher bandwidth services will be left behind in the competitive race.

Flat rate pricing is optimal in encouraging use. Standard works on telecommunications economics usually say nothing about the effect of flat rates on usage. This is obviously not the definitive history of communications. No work could possibly fill that role.

In particular, practically no attention is devoted to technology, regulation, industrial organization, and many other crucial aspects of communication services. Their effects are noted only through the decreasing prices and increasing quality and quantity that users experience. The main themes are growth of communication, the qualitative change this growth produces in how people treat communication, and the evolution of pricing.

The stress is on the user, and in particular on how quality and price differentiation have been used by service providers to influence consumer behaviour. For example, today telegraph company lawyers do not hire people to cut down the poles of a competitor. Also, railroads that compete for the same bottleneck mountain pass do not hire private armies that engage in shooting wars. A more substantial, but related, reason for concentrating on early stages of communication services is that they help clarify the evolution of those services.

The contrasts between the early and mature stages of a technology bring into sharper contrasts the issues of how people treated those services, and what the role of pricing was. The forces that have worked to produce simplicity in pricing in the past are likely to be at least as influential on the Internet. Optimal efficiency will be sacrificed in the interests of satisfying customers.

Further, professionally produced "content" will not be the main factor determining the evolution of the Internet. Communications is likely to grow in revenues and importance, but will do so in often unpredictable ways, as society adopts the new tools to suit its needs. Price indices for the 19th century are rather imprecise, and in any case inflation-adjusted costs do not present an accurate picture of the burden of prices back when living standards were much lower. Therefore some prices are stated in terms of hours of work required to pay that price.

The Internet is widely predicted to produce "digital convergence," in which computing, communications, and broadcasting all merge into a single stream of discrete bits carried on the same ubiquitous network. The popular images of convergence are heavily tinged with the flavour of Hollywood. "Content is king" is the universal buzzword, where content is usually taken to mean professionally prepared material such as books, movies, sports events, or music.

The race is supposedly to determine which organization or alliance will dominate in providing content to the users, ideally in advanced multimedia formats. A recent article concludes that "[the Internet] has become a mass medium used mostly by relatively passive consumers, and as such major content providers will dominate it".

The histories of the telegraph and the telephone show the same pattern. Usually many companies jumped in with unrealistic hopes, most failed, but the industry as a whole prospered. For example, the $187.5 billion of advertising industry revenues pays for almost all television broadcasting, and that provides much of the funding for the movie industry. Further, consumer expenditures on phone services are already contained completely in the general telephone industry figure.

Just the spending on phone services is higher than all advertising outlays. So say good-bye to all those plans for financing the Internet through advertising! Yes, advertising can help fund some services, but it will not provide the generous revenue streams that are needed to support a communications infrastructure as large as the phone system. To obtain the funding that many dot-coms seem to be planning on, it will be necessary to get contributions from more than advertising.

Ecommerce can help, but even that probably will not be enough, and it will be necessary to persuade people to pay for a large chunk of their communications. For example, sales of recorded music come to about $15 billion per year. If one eliminates the overhead costs of the physical distribution system for CDs, one could probably provide the artists with as much money as they make now, and the music labels with as much revenue for their central selection and promotional activities (and their profit) for under half of the $15 billion.

The postal system alone collects almost as much money as the entire movie industry, even though the latter benefits from large foreign sales. For all the publicity it attracts, entertainment is simply not all that large, because people are not willing to pay very much for it. The dream of the early 1990s of financing the "Information Superhighway" through "500 channels to the home on the cable TV network" was an obvious fantasy.

Content is not only a small part of the economy, it is often paid for indirectly. Well over two thirds of newspaper revenues, and almost all of broadcast TV and radio revenues come from advertising. Thus content is being given away in order to attract people to goods and services they are willing to pay for. Although spending for content has been rising, it has been doing so at a sedate pace, and is unlikely to explode.

In particular, consumer spending on content is over 50% higher than on phone services. There is some issue of what one means by content, a question we will return to later. If we take a generous interpretation, we can come up with total content industry revenues comparable to the $256 billion that the telephone industry collected in 1997. However, comparing just the total revenues of those two industries is misleading.

In the case of the telephone industry, the $256 billion does include some service revenues as well as yellow pages advertising, but the overwhelming majority of that money is for simple transport of voice and data. The content industry as a whole, though, has to use its revenues to pay for content as well as the delivery of the content.

The creative souls who command $20 million per movie know their value, and do manage to appropriate a lion's share of the profits from such enterprises, while keeping their risks lower than those of the investors. Similarly, the professionals who compile the Lexis database, or assemble and monitor Reuters' financial data feeds, have to be paid, just like movie actors and musicians.

Hence only some of the revenues of the content industry contribute to the communications infrastructure. That only a fraction of the revenues of the content industry go for delivery is an important point that has analogs in the context of ecommerce. Ecommerce is already big, and is exploding. A dollar of ecommerce transactions does not mean a dollar devoted to the network. Considerably more, but still only around $150 million, went for the servers, software development, and other information technology products and services that are needed to stay competitive in this rapidly changing field.

The contribution of ecommerce to communications is growing, but it has to be kept in perspective. Communications is far from being the largest segment of the economy. It is smaller than cars, housing, food, and especially medicine. It is also about two thirds the size of the primary and secondary education sectors, and comparable to the higher education enterprise. As a fraction of the U.S. economy, it has grown more than 15-fold over the last 150 years.

The predominance of point-to-point communications spending is not new. That has been the historical pattern for ages. For example, in the early 19th century, almost all the revenues of the U.S. postal system came from letters. Yet about as many newspapers as letters were being delivered. The preoccupation of decision makers with content and broadcast communication is also not new.

In the early 19th century, the explicit policy of the U.S. government was to promote wide dissemination of newspapers. They were regarded as the main tool for keeping citizenry informed and engaged in building a unified nation. The policy of the U.S. government to promote newspaper "content" at the expense of person-to-person communication through letters may or may not have been correct.

However, there are reasonable arguments that the preoccupation with newspapers harmed the social and commercial development of the country by stifling circulation of the informal, non-content information that people cared about. In those days, the government understood clearly that what people were willing to pay for was letters, and that newspapers were being subsidized.

However, this differential in willingness to pay does not seem to be understood as well today as it was then. Preoccupation with content has historically been common. For example, it was often thought that one of the principal uses of the telephone would be in broadcasting.

In the end, though, the phone emerged as the prototypical example of point-to-point communication. Radio initially evolved in the other direction. It started out as a point-to-point communication technology, a wireless telegraph. After about two decades of experimentation, it became primarily a broadcast medium.

Further, in the last few decades, with the development of cellular services, radio transmission has started to move back to its roots as a point-to-point communications service. A skeptical reader might say that all this historical stuff is amusing but irrelevant. Studies of the Internet regularly find that Web traffic makes up 60 to 80% of the bytes that are transmitted. Certainly most of the commercial development effort on the Internet and almost all the attention are devoted to content. All argue that the dazzling success of the Web has created a misleading picture of what the Internet is, or is likely to evolve towards.

The content is not king of the Web. Most of the traffic on the Internet is corporate. It is likely that in early 2000, no more than a quarter of the volume went to residential users. Intranet traffic appears to be much less heavily biased towards the Web than that of private individuals.

Furthermore, even the traffic that appears to be Web-based frequently represents a variety of database transactions that are not properly speaking "content." Because browsers are a user-friendly tool that is ubiquitous, a multitude of services have been squeezed into a Web framework, and help perpetuate the image of the Internet as primarily a content-delivery mechanism.

Even if content were king on the Web now, the Web is not king of the Internet. This may again seem absurd, especially in view of the statistics quoted above, that most of the Internet traffic is Web transfers. Content certainly dominated in terms of volume of data.

Newspapers sent by mail weighed about 20 times as much as letters. Further, the density of printed matter is higher than of handwriting, and a typical copy of a newspaper was likely read many more times than a typical letter. Hence newspaper "content" was probably delivering at least a hundred times as much information as letters.

On the Internet in 2000, it is email that is king, even if its volume is small. Today, Web traffic dominates the

Internet in volume, with about 20 times as many bytes as email. Even a decade ago, before the Web, email typically accounted for under 10% of Internet volume. Yet email has been and continues to be the real "killer app" of the Internet.

The ARPANET (the progenitor of the Internet) was built primarily to connect computers. Yet email quickly emerged as the application that mattered the most to users, even in the early days of the network. This was much to the surprise of the system's designers. More recent surveys show that email is still the most valuable service, Ask people whether they would rather give up email or the phone, and the responses will typically be split.

However, when a similar choice is offered between the Web and email, there is no contest. This is true for both individuals and large organizations. Intranets are all the rage, but it is email that makes enterprises run. The perception that content dominates the Internet is fueled by studies such as, which show the winner-take-all phenomenon, with a few sites dominating Web transactions among residential users.

However, one should not read too much into such results. In the early 19th century postal system, studies of usage of information would undoubtedly have reached conclusions similar to those of. Most data from distant locations that people consumed came from newspapers. Further, circulation figures of individual newspapers probably followed the standard Zipf-type distribution, with the most popular papers attracting a disproportionately high fraction of readers.

To re-emphasize the importance of point-to-point communication in the online environment, consider the disappointing reception that WebTV has had. It seems that inexpensive Web browsing is not such a great attraction by itself.

Their inadequate or even totally missing facilities for point-to-point communication appear to have been fatal errors. Next, consider the fates of CompuServe and Prodigy. Set up primarily for database access and online shopping, respectively, both were forced to emphasize communications and are now basically standard ISPs.

The currently most successful of the public online services, AOL, started out as a game network. However, it simply cannot fund anything as large as AOL.) AOL survived and prospered because it was nimble. After several changes in strategy, it partially opened itself up to the Internet. While it has content of its own, and access to the Internet, the majority of the time its subscribers spend online is devoted to email and chat.

By focusing attention on centralized delivery of content, the Web may have prevented a proper appreciation of the importance of the often chaotic and generally unplannable point-to-point communications. The Web and the browsers may have played two main roles. One was to force online service providers to accept an open interoperable standard that made the entire Internet accessible for communications for everyone.

The other was to introduce a user-friendly graphical interface for email, chat, and netnews, which made such communications easier. However, the Web is probably not as important to the Internet as is commonly thought. As an example of the relative value of content and simple pipes, note that the revenues of the entire cable TV industry in 1997 were only slightly higher than for the cell phone carriers.

Yet cell phones currently provide primarily simple, low bandwidth pipes. By early 2000, even the gross revenues of radio telephony exceeded those of the cable TV industry. Further, a large chunk of cable revenues was devoted to paying for content, so in terms of basic network revenues, the cellular industry had pulled ahead even before 1997.

The comparison is even more favourable to low bandwidth wireless pipes when we go outside the U.S. In other industrialized countries, cell phones are often much more widely used, while cable TV penetration is almost always far lower than in the U.S. Thus on a worldwide scale, the comparison is skewed even more heavily against content. The cable TV industry does have excellent prospects for faster growth. However, that growth will surely come more from improved communication capabilities, and less from content.

The general conclusion is that content has been less important than point-to-point communication in the past, including the recent past involving the Internet. Historically, content has often dominated, and probably dominate now. There are arguments, to be presented later, that in the future, content will not provide most of the bits travelling on the Internet.

That content is not king does not mean that content is unimportant in shaping political or social views. The attention paid to writers, and the political advertising on radio and TV, testify to the influence of content. This also is not a new phenomenon.

Content can be profitable. Numerous media companies are doing very well. Content can also be of value to a network, even aside from providing traffic for the network to carry. However, it is probably best to think of content as either catnip or icing on the cake; something to attract new users, or enhance user experience. That is what broadcast TV programs do for the advertisers who pay for them. That may also have been the main role of the Web and browsers in bringing more people to the Internet.

Content is not king does say is that people are willing to pay far more for point-to-point communication than for the famed content. That is likely to be reflected in what kinds of networks are built, and which companies succeed. It inverts the usual ordering of priorities, making point-to-point communication central, and content secondary. The fights over control of movie distribution may be a distraction from the main business of communication.

However, if the consumer places much higher value on personal communication than on content, the case for symmetrical connections becomes stronger. That may mean that fibber to the home may be justified sooner than expected. In the wireless arena, it suggests that for much of the next decade, the best strategy will be to emphasize regular voice transmission, supplemented by email and various low-bandwidth data transfers.

Music and video services are likely to be delayed until much later. In general, content is distributed by "mass" or "broadcast" communications systems. Until a few decades ago, such services could be distinguished easily from "point-to-point" communications, which included first class letters and phone calls, and were specific to the people involved in the transaction. These two types of communications were sometimes combined during distribution, as in the postal system, which carried both letters and newspapers, in an early example of "convergence." However, there was a noticeable distinction in how these two types of communication were prepared, handled, perceived by the recipients, and in how much people were willing to pay for them.

During the last few decades, the distinction between point-to-point and broadcast communication began to blur. Computers allowed for the mass preparation of personalized letters offering credit cards, say. Answering machines and voice response systems led to machine-mediated point-to-point communications.

Many of the standard phone calls access just such services, and the Internet is leading to increasing usage of them. These types of interactions will flourish on the Internet, and some will be merging with content, but they are more typical of the standard point-to-point communications. One of the main lessons from the history of communications is that technologies are often adopted rapidly, but seldom at the astronomical rates that popular imagination associates with the Internet. This applies even to the Internet, where change tends to be less rapid than is often thought.

Browsers were adopted rapidly. The first informal release of Mosaic took place in the spring of 1993, and in under two years, the majority of Internet traffic was Web-related. However, that was an exception. Other changes have been slower. Just consider Internet telephony, introduced back in 1995. It is finally beginning to have a noticeable effect, but it is far from dominant.

In general, the time a new technology takes to become widespread has not changed much in the last half century. Even technologies with compelling advantages tend to take a decade to dominate markets. Fax machines took about 10 years, from the introduction of the first inexpensive models until they became ubiquitous. Cell phones, one of the fastest growing industries, have taken about 15 years to reach their.

Cable TV has taken three decades to reach about 60% of U.S. households. Music CDs and more recently DVDs show similar patterns, taking on the order of a decade to reach dominance. Aside from the unusually rapid ascendency of the browser-Web combination, fast change is usually associated with the presence of forcing agents. These can be either governments or a small number of key decision makers who can shift an industry's direction. An example of such forcing agents are the information technology managers at large banks and other enterprises.

A transition of voice phone traffic from circuit switched transmission to the Internet might occur rapidly for just this reason. The carriers might be able to implement it rapidly, since it could be done essentially invisibly to the end users, and the decisions would need to be made by only a few people. The decade-long diffusion periods listed above for consumer goods and services are due to the inertia of the millions of people who have to individually decide to adopt a new technology.

Most new products and services are in that category. Sociological changes are even slower, taking a generation or two. Normal change, with a simple shift in technology that offers serious advantages over older, more established competitor, takes on the order of a decade. The speed with which new technologies diffuse has a direct relevance for the question of whether content might be king of the Internet. It is possible to make a case that even if content is not king now, it might be king in the future, when convergence does occur. Some evidence for this can be derived from the comparison of cable TV and cell phone industries. Their revenues and growth rates were cited as demonstrating that point-to-point communication is more important than content.

If convergence moves delivery of most of the content to the Internet, and transport grabs two thirds of the total revenues from content, then the network will get a huge new source of revenue. Total content spending in the U.S. is comparable to that on the phone system, so two thirds of that would make a huge difference to network financing. This scenario is not totally implausible, since the current content distribution system is grossly inefficient.

The Internet offers a chance to reduce some of the inefficiencies of the current system. For the current dominant content producers, the real threat from the Internet is probably less from piracy, and more from disintermediation. New producers can come in and, unburdened by the high overheads and obsolete habits of established players, can offer better deals to both the creative talent and the consumers.

The Internet is a disruptive technology, it does have unprecedented ability to emulate other delivery mechanisms, and we are already seeing rapid growth in music delivery on it. As an example of what can happen to even the most solid-seeming businesses, just consider the Encyclopaedia Britannica. In spite of having the greatest brand name and by far the best content in the encyclopedia field, it has been floundering, and has yet to find a viable business model.

Thus dramatic changes are indeed possible in the electronic environment. Still, there are other, more substantial, arguments against the content thesis. The Internet will surely have a major impact on the content industries. However, as was discussed above, consumers are slow to change their behavior. Even the Encyclopaedia Britannica has had a decade in which to flounder.

Even in the business environment, adoption of new technologies that require a thorough re-engineering of all internal processes is slow. The business-to-consumer dot-coms have discovered this already, and the business-to-business ones are in the process of learning. Although we are living in the Internet era, fundamental change is not all that much faster than a century and a half ago.

Slow adoption of new technologies means that convergence will be spread over a decade or more, and there will be continuing competition from traditional media, as well as increasing diversity of delivery mechanisms for content. This may mean that the writers and artists will get a bigger share of the pie. That appears to have been the trend over the last few decades, with movie actors and professional sport stars increasing their share of the revenues their work brings in.

There will certainly be a shift of revenue towards broadband services, but content distribution may not be the largest contributor to it. The main reason to question whether content will ever make giant contributions to network costs is that by the time convergence is likely to occur, at least a decade into the future, content transmission is likely to be a small fraction of total traffic.

Further, most content will probably be distributed as ordinary file transfers, not in real-time mode. High prices could be charged for content distribution if content made up most of the traffic, or else if content required special transmission quality. Since neither of these conditions is likely to be satisfied, though, content will probably constitute just some of the huge number of large files, many encrypted, that will be flying around the network.

Internet backbone traffic appears to be about doubling each year. Further, advances in photonics and additional fiber deployment appear to allow for a doubling of network capacity each year for the next decade. In early 2000, Internet backbone traffic in the U.S. appeared to be less than a third of voice traffic in volume, but is likely to become larger by about 2002, with the transition point slightly later for the rest of the world. However, if voice traffic were to be packetized, it would almost surely be compressed, and then its volume would already be less than that of Internet traffic.

Broadcast TV would still overwhelm the Internet of the year 2000, but at 100% annual growth rates, it will not be too long before there is more than enough capacity to provide a high quality video channel for every person on Earth. This is because bandwidth that is likely to be required to satisfy any single person's real-time transmission needs will not be increasing fast.

The versions of Moore's Law that hold in different industries operate at diverse rates. Microprocessors are doubling in computing power every 18 to 24 months, while fiber transmission capacity is doubling every year. On the other hand, display technology is advancing extremely slowly.

Broadcast TV resolution has been static for several decades, and even the planned move to HDTV will require only a modest increase in bandwidth. Thus satisfying the needs for real-time multimedia transmission will not require much of the Internet's capacity.

Content is likely to form only a small fraction of Internet traffic for reasons explained. In addition, real-time delivery of content is likely to be an even smaller factor, for reasons discussed in much greater detail in. Transmission capacity is approximately doubling each year, which is a much faster rate of improvement than Moore's Law for semiconductors. However, hard disk storage capacity is also about doubling each year. Furthermore, that capacity is already huge.

At the beginning of 2000, the U.S. Internet backbones appeared to be carrying about 12,000 TB (terabytes) of traffic each month. However, the total world hard disk capacity was 3,000,000 TB. Thus it would take about 20 years to transmit all the data on those disks over U.S. Internet backbones. The presence of huge local storage capacity in local PCs or cable TV setup boxes will make it much more attractive to send even content as files, not as real time transmissions.

There will be a growing volume for real time multimedia traffic, for applications such as videoconferencing. However, such applications are likely to be swamped by ordinary file transfers. The dominant mode of operation is likely to be fast download to local storage, fast transfer to whatever display device one wishes to use (often a mobile information appliance), and then playback. That is already the model we see emerging with MP3, Napster, and TiVo. The advantages of this model include the ability to implement it now, before the Internet can be made ready for real-time streaming media. It also accommodates gracefully the forecasted explosive growth in small mobile devices, which will often have small storage and low bandwidth over wireless links, and thus will be most useful if they can get data from local storage. This model also allows for easy integration with special hardware for intellectual property protection.

That real-time multimedia traffic would not dominate the Internet has been predicted several times in the past. It is an obvious conclusion from the rapid increase in traffic. The huge volume of local storage will surely stimulate the generation of non-content traffic. Both corporations and individuals so far have had no difficulty filling their disks with data. For firms, various databases will likely continue to proliferate and grow.

For residential users, pictures are the leading candidates for filling those disks. Ease of use, lower cost, and instant gratification all stimulate use, and digital camera owners appear to be taking many more pictures than they ever did with regular film. The same electronic technology that is producing better disks and processors is also producing better cameras.

Historically, it appears that privately taken pictures have traditionally been the dominant source of data. Email and the Web may not be flexible enough. Yet the most successful communication technologies, the mail and the telephone, reached their full potential only when they embraced sociability and those "useless calls" as their goal. That seemingly idle chitchat not only provided direct revenues, but it encouraged the diffusion of the corresponding technology, and made it more useful for commercial and other applications.

Such social interaction frequently function to grease the wheels of commerce. This work is largely the story of the development of the communications infrastructure from the point of view of the user. Usually an infrastructure is noted for being unnoticed; it is simply there, something we come to rely upon, do not have to think much about, and are horribly inconvenienced when it malfunctions.

Electricity, water, mail, and the phone are excellent examples. Yet they all took much effort to reach this stage. The key failing of the telegraph, as is detailed in later sections, is that it never became a true infrastructure component. It was a revolutionary technology, the "Victorian Internet," as one writer has called it, but it was too cumbersome and too expensive to attract much usage, and in particular never carried much of that "useless" social traffic that pushed the mail and the telephone to their eminent positions.

Traditionally, commercial users have subsidized residential ones. Sometimes this was done even involuntarily, as in higher rates dictated by carriers or by government regulators, and sometimes voluntarily, as in paying for toll-free 800 numbers. One of the purposes of this work is to examine the history of such subsidies. It appears probable that they will also play a large role on the Internet.

The value of a broadcast network is usually regarded as proportional to the number of users in it. On the other hand, a point-to-point communication network is often said, by Metcalfe's Law, to have value proportional to the square of the number of member. This then leads to the conclusion that eventually, once a single network like the Internet reaches a large enough size, point-to-point communications will provide much higher value than broadcast.

With value proportional to the number of users, there would be few inherent advantages to an open network. The sum of the values of several completely or partially separate networks would be the same as of a unified network. On the other hand, if point-to-point communications were to dominate, and if Metcalfe's Law were to hold, there would be strong economic incentives to a unified network without barriers.

The Internet has done quite well without content, and can continue to flourish without it. Content will have a place on the Internet, possibly a substantial place. However, its place will likely be subordinate to that of business and personal communication. The explosive rise of the Internet is only the most recent chapter in a remarkable history of humanity becoming increasingly connected, the "annihilation of space and time," in a phrase going back at least to the early 19th century.

However, growth rates rivaling that of the Internet have been observed occasionally before, for example in the development of the telegraph. The wireless industry is experiencing similar growth even now. A related one is to avoid the complexities of trying to measure the volume of information delivered by broadcast media. With point-to-point communication, it has often been true that the entire content was read, heard, or seen by the recipient. With broadcast communication, accounting is harder.

The communications industry as a whole has been expanding for centuries. Not only that, but most of the prominent services have continued growing. The tables in this section provide more eloquent testimony to this historical fact than words can. Even the venerable mail, often derisively called "snail mail," is still growing.

Although there have been many predictions that mail would decline as a result of competition from the telegraph, the telephone, and more recently from email, it has continued to expand. Various new services have been added, such as money orders, home delivery, and parcel post. Even without the new services, the volume of letters alone has been increasing. Overall, total mail volume and spending have grown at impressive rates. Even in recent years prices have been decreasing, if we adjust them for increases in earnings. Moreover, this was not an isolated case of a frontier economy getting civilized.

In France, the postal system revenues are more than three times larger as a fraction of GDP than they were 150 years. In spite of this, mail is no longer the dominant communication technology, as it is dwarfed by the phone industry. Comparison of tables 3.1 and 3.4 shows the telephone passed the mail in revenues by 1920, and today is about four times as large. Adding the contributions of these two industries, we find that their role in the economy, measured as a fraction of GDP, has increased almost 20-fold over the last 150 years, from 0.2% to over 3.5%.

The tide of increasing communications volumes has been powerful enough to lift most services. The telegraph did not stop the mail from growing. The telephone took a long time to eliminate the telegraph. Wireless telephony and the Internet have been growing explosively, yet wired telephony is still growing. Even fax use is increasing. Yet if anything should have been eliminated by the Internet, it surely should have been the fax.

Most messages sent by fax are typeset on a computer, printed out, and then fed into a fax machine.

Still, the fax is ubiquitous, inexpensive, easy to use, and provides some features, such as signatures, that the Internet can and will eventually provide, but does not offer now. A technology that survived for longer than the fax is the electric telegraph. One can speculate that had the telephone not been invented, the telegraph might have spread more widely and become less expensive.

Eventually it might have developed into something like our Internet, going from digital transmission directly to digital, bypassing the analog phone stage. There was intense development of new applications of telegraph technology in the second half of the 19th century for stock tickers as well as fire and home alarms. However, these developments came to nought.

The telephone started encroaching on the bread and butter business of the telegraph, and the latter could not compete effectively. The long survival of the telegraph suggests many lessons about rates of technological change. The Internet can emulate other communication technologies much better than the phone could emulate the telegraph, say. Still, the power of inertia should not be underestimated. The general progression for new technologies has been to start as an expensive and limited service. Then, as a result of technological improvements as well as economies of scale, prices usually declined and utilization increased. Growth in usage was accomplished by development of new types of usage.

Some communication technologies, such as the electric telegraph and the telephone, went into public service right from the start. Initial usage was typically limited to special high-value commercial communications, since prices were high. In the Introduction, the sending of a letter in early 19th century

England was compared (on the basis of earnings) to the purchase of a book today, costing about two hours of work.

Telephone service initially was also extremely expensive. For example, a century ago, unlimited local service in New York City cost $20 per month. That is comparable to $2,000 per month currently, when one considers prices in relation to average earnings. The precise economic benefits of communication are a complicated subject beyond the scope of this work. However, they have consistently been high, often demonstrably so.

The main reason telecommunications services are being liberalized and privatized around the world is to spur innovation and greater investments. Many careful studies have been conducted that documented the contribution of communications to speeding up economic growth. These benefits are easily appreciated by individuals.

A century ago, the highest penetration of phone service in the U.S. was in the Midwestern farming states. Even when there were no direct monetary savings, the savings in time from not making unneeded trips or arriving right on time were immense, and easy to understand for anyone. Once mail and phone service prices became low enough, social uses exploded. This enabled those two industries to increase their shares of the economy.

The telegraph never moved beyond the high-priced and infrequent commercial use stage, and eventually died. The large and often immediately noticeable economic effects of communications meant that any changes in availability or pricing of services could have a large effect on the economy. Even regular mail played such a role.

Much of the maneuvering in the U.S. Congress in the first half of the 19th century over postal rates had to do with the competitive positions of newspaper publishers in small towns versus those in large ones, and those in the South versus those in the Northeast. The interaction of mail with economic life developed gradually. This was largely because mail evolved gradually, and was a familiar service, simply performing better and less expensively what everyone could do, namely carry letters at the speed people could travel.

Postal services did play a major role in the economy even in the early 19th century. However, mail was apparently not associated in the public eye with dramatic changes, at least not negative ones. The electric telegraph introduced a novel phenomenon.

The Internet is sometimes portrayed as a uniquely potent disruptive technology. Yet it is worth keeping in mind that the electric telegraph had a similar effect. In many ways, the telegraph was a greater innovation than the Internet. It was the first technology that effectively separated communication from transportation. It had a dramatic effect on science and technology, and it facilitated huge economic changes.

The role of the telegraph in transforming the economy of the 19th century can be illustrated briefly by considering the history of the Rothschild banking dynasty. They were the world's largest financiers of railroads in the middle of the 19th century, and much of their wealth derived from that source. On the other hand, they were hostile to the telegraph, since it eroded their competitive advantage.

In the first half of the 19th century, the Rothschilds attained unprecedented dominance of international finance because they alone had a cohesive organization covering all the major financial centres of Europe. The closely knit family could trust each other, and in addition they had a private communicaticn system that provided them with news in advance of rivals.

Most businesses in the mid-19th century had a choice of using the telegraph or dying, and using it effectively often meant large changes in modes of operation. This new technology was closely associated with new industries, especially the railroads, and new styles of management. It did lead to much more centralized control in both government and business affairs.

The establishment of a direct telegraph line between England and India in 1870 was an event of far-reaching importance. The delay in communication was a great advantage to the Government of India in so far as it of necessity left the initiation of policy in urgent matters to its own hands, and enabled it to confront the Secretary of State with accomplished facts. But all this was bound to change when the Secretary of State had to be kept constantly informed of the course of events in India, and was in a position to issue immediate orders.

There is not doubt that the telegraph and the telephone had a great role in transforming society. However, many of the claims of dramatic changes caused by new communication technologies should be treated with caution. Corporate management was centralized, but there was an explosion in ranks of corporations, so some general measure of autonomy by managers may well have increased.

Many communication technologies led to predictions that they would lead to a new era of universal brotherhood and peace. For example, the International Telegraph Union, was the first permanent international technical organization. There have been many predictions that the Internet would doom large corporations.

In the absence of such costs, the factory worker, the garbage collector, the secretary, the software developer, and the salesman could just contract for their contributions to any given job in a decentralized market, without the need for a cumbersome bureaucracy. Since the Internet reduces transaction costs, it has often been predicted that it would eliminate the need for large organizations, and reduce the world to cottage enterprises.

The same phenomenon occurred in the second half of the 19th century, facilitated by the lower transaction and coordination costs offered by the telegraph. There does seem to be a strong tendency today to move away from vertical integration. That mode of operation appears to be replaced by enterprises concentrated in narrower horizontal layers of the economy, but operating on a worldwide scale.

New technologies have often facilitated changes, but they were seldom the sole factors. Precise predictions have seldom been correct. Society has adopted the tools that were offered to it in a variety of often unexpected ways. The one factor that is undeniable, though, is that apparent from the tables in this section.

Historically communication has been extremely highly valued. Individuals and enterprises have been devoting increasingly large fractions of their resources to it, and consuming rapidly rising volumes of it. The growth in volume of information has led to a change in how we react to it. Over the last two centuries we have moved from scarcity to surfeit. There have always been some complaints about too much information.

There are many worries that restrictive copyright laws will limit our access to data. However, in practice what we can see is an unprecedented abundance of information. With reduced marginal costs of distribution, content providers are fighting for eyeballs. Until a few years ago, you had to pay for a subscription to the New York Times, and also had to wait, often a long time, for your copy to be delivered. Today, you can get it for free on the Web soon after the editors decide on the final layout. When communication opportunities were rare, and transmission slow, it was natural that great care was taken with correspondence.

New communication technologies require new modes of acceptable usage. Today people complain about rudeness of cell phone users in restaurants or on airplanes, and wonder at the strange sights of cell phone users with headsets who seem to be talking to themselves. The phone also required development of new rules of etiquette.

Even the wider use of mail for social communication led to "a burgeoning market for how-tomanuals to teach ordinary Americans the once-arcane custome of maintaining a correspondence with distant friends and family". For a communication service provider, the task is to make life for the customer as painless as possible. A seamless integration of the Internet into people's lives should be the goal.

The Internet is the latest addition to the communication infrastructure that has been developing over the centuries. Most of the discussion in this work is limited to the 19th and 20th centuries. That was the period when the modern industrialized world was born, when the basic power, water, transportation, as well as communications infrastructures were built.

Many similarities between the Internet and earlier communications services have been noted in earlier sections, and many more are presented in this one and later ones. However, there are also numerous similarities to other services, as well as common themes running through the combined history of all of them. For example, today's carpal tunnel syndrome was known in the late 19th century as "glass arm" or "telegrapher's cramp".

As an example, most new technologies led to new forms of crime, and certainly to fears of crime. In late 1999 and early 2000, denial of service attacks on the Internet as well as other, real or potential problems, led to concerns that anonymity on the Internet might be harmful. The electric telegraph in France was initially limited to government use. Similarly, to prevent criminal elements from 'using the telegraph to hatch their detestable plots with more ease and rapidity', the law demanded that private dispatches be sent un-coded and signed, and that the user declare his or her identity.

A common feature of all communication services has been that prices have usually had only a slight relation to costs. Average prices have, over long periods, decreased in line with the decline in costs. However, the structure of prices has traditionally included cross-subsidies. It is often difficult to tell when such subsidies exist. One could hope that at least the the economics of postal systems would be well understood. These systems are large, relatively slowly changing, and unusually open to public scrutiny.

The prominence of the Internet has tended to overshadow the rise of another great high-tech suc-cess, namely that of the wireless industry. There are more users of cell phones in the world than there are Internet users. Cell phones are a nice counterexample to the claim that is sometimes heard that metered services cannot grow fast. Wireless services have been growing rapidly, but have been metered from the beginning, and rates remain high. The U.S. cell phone industry collects on average about $0.25 per minute of wireless calls, as compared to $0.10 per minute for the wired long distance phone service. The widely varying costs of wired and radio transmission are reflected in the universal use of compression for voice calls over cell phones.

In recent years, as costs of transmission have decreased, use of compression even on very long underwater links has decreased. The slight disadvantages in complexity, delay, and so on that compression introduces have more than compensated for the substantial bandwidth savings that it offers. This is a nice example of how simplicity has triumphed over efficiency.

On the other hand, compression on the radio link reflects the scarcity of bandwidth in that environment. Improvements in technology and greater spectrum allocations for communications will increase radio bandwidth. Still, this bandwidth is likely to remain orders of magnitude lower than that available on fiber optic backbones. Hence, even in the long run, although there may be plenty of bandwidth for voice calls, there will be a shortage for data, as mobile devices with powerful processors attempt to connect to big photonics pipes over relatively narrow radio channels.

Multimedia "content" will likely not be a major factor for many years. On the other hand, it seems that the prospects are excellent for stimulating much greater voice calling, since cell phones are used far less than wired ones. Digital messaging can be very useful in that regard. The scarcity of wireless bandwidth and its high price argue for quality and price differentiation. However, little of either is visible in the cellular industry.

In the U.S., the cell phone owner pays for incoming calls. This imposes the risk of high charges not under the control of the user, and induces most people to keep their cell phones turned off except when they wish to make a call. The industry is trying to move to a "calling party pays" policy, but progress in that direction has been slow so far. Even if subscribers do not have to pay for incoming calls, other barriers will remain.

Today, however, it might be better to raise the price of headsets, to move closer to a flat rate pricing system. Not making a subscriber pay for incoming calls is likely to stimulate usage. Not making that user pay for outgoing calls is likely to be even more effective. Each wired phone is used for almost an hour each day in the U.S., far more than in other countries.

Broadband Demand

Broadband—high-speed, always—on Internet connectivity—represents the next phase in the evolution of the Internet. Most experts predict broadband will enable applications and services that transform our economy, education, health-care, R&D, homeland security, military effectiveness, entertainment, government and the quality of life for citizens around the world. The deployment and usage of broadband will significantly impact the global competitiveness of nations and businesses in the future. Not surprisingly, many nations, states, cities and communities are trying to accelerate the deployment and usage of broadband networks. To date, these efforts have predominantly focused on the supply side—promoting infrastructure build—out and determining appropriate competition and regulatory policies. Since the primary role of government economic policy is to set an environment that encourages capital formation, rewards risk and encourages competition, investment and innovation, supply side inquiries remain vitally important. Supply side decisions are also critical because we'll need significant upgrades of existing network infrastructure to supply the last mile bandwidth required for advanced applications -today's broadband will be tomorrow's traffic jam, and the need for speed will persist as new applications and services gobble up existing bandwidth.

Broadband Applications

The following parts highlights the myriad ways in which broadband can, or is predicted to, transform the economy, education, health-care, R&D, homeland security, the military, and the quality of life for seniors and those with disabilities, among others. These possibilities make clear that there is no shortage of 'killer' applications in the pipeline, and their impacts are likely to be very significant. As these services and applications become available, they will drive broadband and justify the investment for citizens, businesses and governments. At the outset, however, it is worth observing that broadband alone has minimal impact. Businesses simply switching to high-speed access will not suddenly save millions of dollars or begin producing more competitive goods or services. Likewise, consumers should not expect instantly better lives or more fulfilling relationships just because they signed up for broadband. Broadband is an incredible enabling technology. It allows businesses that are willing to embrace Internet business solutions to transform business processes and realize significant returns on investment. It offers consumers new opportunities to work or learn more productively (at their desks or from home), publish multimedia, switch from viewers of entertainment to participants, and - most importantly -dramatically expand their communication possibilities. But these transformations are not always plug-and-play solutions - they often take work and effort. That said, the following broadband-enabled applications should ensure widespread deployment and justify efforts to stimulate growth.

Promoting jobs, productivity and sustained growth economists are already predicting significant macroeconomic benefits from the proliferation of broadband networks. It is believed that widespread broadband usage can extend the IT revolution and further improve national and regional productivity, helping to promote robust economic growth and increase our standard of living. In the most extensive economic study of broadband to-date, economists at the Brookings Institution estimate widespread, high-speed broadband access will increase our national GDP by $500 billion annually by 2006.

Due to broadband technologies are so new (and continue to evolve), there are no definitive studies of their actual impact on regional economic growth and tech- led economic development. Of course that never prevents economists and technologists from speculating or estimating. Specific regional economic development benefits anticipated as a result of greater broadband deployment and usage include:

— *Job creation and retention:* Broadband availability allows local businesses to remain competitive, operate more efficiently, and access more consumers more quickly and thus grow faster. Smaller manufacturers need access to high-speed networks to remain part of the supply chain of larger players.

— Reduced traffic congestion and automotive pollution through increased telecommuting.

— *More successful industrial growth, recruitment and retention.* Information businesses can start and locate anywhere they want, and they tend to look for areas with educated workforces, advanced infrastructures and high quality of life. Knowledge workers expect and require advanced telecommunications infrastructure.

— *Improved K-12 education systems:* The surface of technology-based improvements to education and have miles to go. Today's children are oft en immersed in digital technologies their entire lives except when they're at school, where technology is inadequately used. Integrated into learning by trained teachers, broadband connections can improve education for students.

— *More productive research and development:* A July 2002 Technology Administration roundtable on

'BioCenters of Excellence' heard from several biotech and economic development leaders that high bandwidth connectivity is critical to advanced biotechnology research and database access.

— *Increased start-up and entrepreneurial activities:* The Internet enables entrepreneurship, facilitates networking critical to funding start- ups and encourages rapid tech-led economic growth, with broadband empowering smaller players to compete against larger and more established companies.

— *Urban core revitalization:* In cities around the nation, broadband-enabled cyber districts are transforming large blocks of formerly empty warehousing and manufacturing space into highly sought-after post-industrial hubs.

— Improved government efficiencies and service delivery through e- government.

Certainly the deployment of broadband will be critical to establishing markets for the next generation of high tech equipment. Increasing the speed and capacity of data networks will enable innovations in semiconductors, applications, computers, communications equipment and devices, driving the next wave of technology investment. In addition, greater usage of advanced Internet should help the economy more quickly absorb the extraordinary excess capacity that resulted from the technology spending boom of the late 1990's. The great hope of the distressed telecom and telecom equipment sectors is that increased capacity in last-mile networks will allow greater usage of untapped long-haul capacity and generate revenue opportunities through new services.

Broadband and education

New technologies are bringing hope and opportunity to those who need them most. Just begun to scratch the surface of possibilities for using the Internet to improve learning and education, as 14 visionaries convened by the Technology Administration recently predicted. The more-than 200 Universities connected to Internet2 are experimenting with unprecedented collaborations among researchers and multinational, cross-continent classrooms. Congress' Web-Based Education Commission reported in December 2000 that broadband connectivity is a critical element of using information technology to transform and improve education. And online education/training in the workplace is also growing extremely quickly and becoming increasingly sophisticated with widespread broadband in the business sector. Rapid advancements in the years ahead could enable new learning environments that employ simulations, visualizations, immersive environments, game playing, intelligent tutors and avatars, networks of learners, reusable building blocks of content, and more.

The technologies that are coming could permit rich and compelling learning opportunities that meet all learners' needs, and provide knowledge and training when and where it is needed, all the while boosting the productivity of learning and lowering its cost. The Technology Administration is convening a summit on the potential for advanced technologies to transform education and learning later this month, and the experts clearly expect future innovations in learning technologies to ride and rely on high-speed networks.

Broadband networks present enormous opportunities for life sciences and health care. More than access to medical information and online pharmacies, the real promise of telemedicine envisions citizens getting home check- ups without long drives and long waits, and anytime, anywhere diagnoses. Blood analysis devices in the home could permit online assessments of cholesterol and enzyme levels, anticipating problems before they require an ambulance. High-speed wireless connections could allow 24-7 monitoring of patients without confining them to hospital beds, while rural and remote doctors might be able to obtain second opinions from the world's foremost experts. Broadband-based applications such as robotic surgery and remote diagnosis could allow American doctors to answer the President's call for volunteerism by helping others in need around the world without leaving home.

In July 2002, the Technology Administration at the Department of Commerce hosted an expert roundtable to explore issues of innovation, demand and investment in telemedicine. Experts advised that broadband-enabled telehealth applications offer opportunities to better prevent diseases and provide health care, empower patients and doctors, reduce medical errors, reduce costs and prepare for disasters, although significant policy, regulatory and coordination barriers must be overcome to achieve to more robust telemedicine usage. We hope to issue a more thorough report on telemedicine in the coming months, but one thing is clear—the most promising telemedicine applications need serious bandwidth.

Broadband and the global war

Transforming the Military Broadband is also core critical

to another of the President's top priorities—winning the global war on terrorism. Broadband boosters should take hope from military efforts to develop and improve information techno logy systems, since applications created originally for defense purposes regularly become commercialized and available for civilian use (as did the Internet itself). There may be no better example of an organization undergoing IT-enabled business process transformation that the United States military. Post-Cold War, post-Gulf War forces are becoming more mobile and more accurate—light and lethal - increasing effectiveness while decreasing the likelihood of U.S. casualties or civilian collateral damage. The technological core underlying these new systems—from unmanned reconnaissance aircraft, to data links among soldiers on the battlefield, to more efficient procurement systems—is a broadband data network.

The high-speed Internet promises to extend new possibilities to those facing traditional limitations. A recent report for the National Association of the Deaf observes that broadband-enabled remote interpreting and peer-to-peer signing offer radical opportunities for the deaf.

For seniors, broadband can enhance communications with family and friends, expand opportunities for lifelong learning, improve delivery of health care services, support independent living, and create new options for entertainment and interaction with the government. And as video email messages replace written text on a true broadband Internet, communications opportunities may greatly expand for the millions of illiterate Americans presently challenged by text-based Internet communications.

With such extraordinary possibilities, robust broadband demand and usage seems inevitable. Yet many leaders understandably wish to accelerate broadband uptake to realize its benefits more rapidly. To determine the best ways to accelerate broadband usage, one must understand the current market trends in broadband demand.

The most obvious factor limiting broadband demand today is cost. The dial- up consumers why they were not upgrading to broadband networks found 72% of respondents complaining broadband was 'too expensive.' Many consumers fail to see the value proposition for investing in broadband, considering it a luxury they cannot afford or not yet worth the $45-$55 per month investment. Some consumers believe that broadband is a workplace technology with little value outside the office (and little interest in bringing work home). Gartner Group predicted that only 10% of households in France, Germany, and the UK will have broadband access by 2005 unless prices fall. These sentiments appear to be exacerbated by concerns over price instability - 91% of all broadband providers (that did not go bankrupt in 2001) increased price since the beginning of 2001, by an average of 11.4% for DSL and 16% for cable.

Yet even if broadband were free, one should not expect to see 100% usage immediately, as is demonstrated by an experiment being conducted 65 miles southwest of downtown Atlanta. In LaGrange, Georgia, the city is partnering with Charter Communications to offer cable broadband access at almost zero cost for all interested consumers (including WebTV for those without PCs). One year after first unveiling this offer, only 29% of citizens had subscribed (down from 49%

during the period of heavy promotion). City leaders suggest barriers to greater adoption include reluctance to embrace change (often generational), lack of relevant local content, lack of reading ability, and lack of appreciation for the possibilities made available by broadband access. It is worth noting that reluctance to embrace new technology is hardly just an American, generational or rural phenomenon. According to research from Computer Weekly reported in February 2002, 72% of UK consumers expressed no interest in paying for broadband Internet access.

Content is king. A majority of consumers will sign up for broadband when value-adding applications and services are readily available, easily understood, and offered at reasonable prices. Wildly popular services and applications drove adoption of earlier technologies—e.g., fax machine (legal fax signatures), the PC (spreadsheets), and the dial-up Internet (email, web browser) - and they will be the key to accelerating broadband deployment as well. The good news is that, for consumers, we already know some of these killer apps. Right now the most significant driver for consumer broadband adoption has been telework—the ability for consumers to work from home more readily. According to In-Stat/MDR, more than 60% of the US workforce is in remote locations, an enormous potential source for future broadband teleworkers.

In addition to concerns over price and (lack of sufficiently compelling) content, would-be broadband consumers express concern over deployment hassles and lack of plug-and-play equipment. Stories of dissatisfaction with service providers are legion, with some complaining that companies make you wait at home all day or require multiple trips to install the technology effectively. These inconveniences appear to influence narrowband consumers' decisions to not adopt broadband, and broadband consumers' spending decisions. In a 2002 study commissioned by Motive Communications :

— 51% of respondents using broadband claimed that they had encountered problems with service and support, such as having to contact a provider multiple times to get a problem solved or unacceptable delays in support.

— 90% of US broadband users said they didn't have enough confidence to purchase additional services from their current provider.

It is worth noting, however, that in the long-term, broadband access is likely to sell precisely because it offers greater conveniences for consumers. Home networking technologies, such as 802. wireless, offer blockbuster appeal for entertainment and teleworking. Parks Associates found that over 50% of American Internet households are interested in networking digital entertainment content among PCs, TVs, stereos and DVD players. Of course the success of these technologies in driving broadband demand will depend upon their reliability, security, ease of installation, compatibility with legacy consumer electronics and consumers' continuing ability to attach them to the network.

The fourth area most clearly impacting demand for higher-speed Internet access is consumer confidence. Consumers are concerned about privacy, security, SPAM and unsavory online locations - the dark side of the Net. Despite the fact that 99% of the most heavily trafficked

Web sites post privacy policies, a June 2002 study from Jupiter Media Metrix indicated that almost 70% of US consumers worry that their privacy is at risk online. Consumer fears over security—including identity theft, hackers, fraud-artists and viruses—are even more pronounced. A July 2002 Gartner Research study found that 30% of those currently using the Web to shop on a regular basis said they would stop using the Internet for purchases if they lost $25 [to fraud], while 58% of non-regular Internet shoppers said that a loss of less than $25 would keep them from purchasing anything else on the Web. Consumers are likewise deterred from greater Internet use by difficulties escaping the unsavory side of the Internet, including pornographic materials. Unsolicited email from adult-oriented Web sites increased 450% from June 2001 to June 2002 according to Cyber Atlas, and the omnipresence of porn sites keeps some folks off the Internet entirely.

Broadband Demand in Businesses

As with consumers, businesses are steadily signing up for high-speed access and implementing broadband business solutions. Many businesses are using broadband to improve business processes or achieve efficiencies. Others are migrating to Internet-based systems to remain part of the supply chain of larger organizations that have moved their procurement systems online. Telecommuting is driving significant business upgrades to broadband, according a September 2002 report to In-Stat/MDR, as businesses look for secure solutions to link remote offices and increasingly mobile workers. Yet as with consumers, several factors limit the pace with which companies are upgrading to broadband. Similar to consumers, businesses are motivated by concerns over cost, convenience / ease-of-use, and confidence in the security of online environments. With respect to content, there is arguably a richer array of business applications than consumer applications already out there. However, many businesses—especially small businesses—don't understand or appreciate what high-speed Internet access is or what broadband applications can do for them.

The business awareness barriers were reiterated by experts at a March 25, 2002 roundtable held by the Technology Administration. Business leaders from NFIB, the U.S. Chamber of Commerce and the National Association of Manufacturers, among others, reported that companies often:

— Fail to see the return on investment (value proposition) for broadband upgrades, especially in a challenging business environment.

— Fear they lack skilled experts at the firm to manage the networks and run the applications.

— Need more strategic advice from their suppliers.

— Lack management commitment to the Internet as a key part of the business strategy.

— Don't perceive demand among their consumer base.

Are concerned about security, privacy and other legal considerations. More than 20% of companies surveyed by In-Stat/MDR indicated they would not chose any type of broadband for their main office location, while 70% of respondents said 'security' and 'hosted applications' were key influencers for their firm's main office bandwidth requirements.

States and localities around the U.S. are also taking steps to promote broadband demand. Some of these initiatives include:

Considering Bandwidth when addressing issues such as rights of way, taxes and application fees, tower siting, zoning, building and construction codes, building access, franchise agreements, historic preservation and environmental protections. For example, the state of Michigan recently enacted legislation to establish a level regulatory playing field for all telecommunications and information carriers, enacting one-stop right-of-way permitting system to create common rules for all carriers and establishing a single tax and fee system to replace differing systems around the state. Aggregating Demand to incent carrier deployment, as is being done by entities such as Berkshire Connect in New England. The Technology Administration is partnering with the Appalachian Regional Commission on a series of events to promote understanding of successful demand aggregation strategies.

Deploying eGovernment: As in LaGrange, citizens want content relevant to their lives, such as community information and local government services. For example, Franklin County (OH) auditor Joseph Testa allows citizens to renew dog licenses or access geographic information about property lines / water lines / etc. on his web site—value-adding information addressing local concerns.

Industry trade associations and business leaders are also taking steps that appear to promote broadband demand. Such efforts include, among other things:

Promoting Business and Consumer Understanding: The Positively Broadband campaign offers a good example of private sector leadership to promote awareness and understanding of the benefits of broadband. Likewise, SeniorNet is working to educate senior citizens about what broadband can mean for them.

Forging Partnerships Between Broadband Creators and Business Users: The Information Technology Industry Council and NFIB have announced intentions to work together to promote broadband deployment and demand. Opportunities for technology creators to work with their customers on improving awareness of applications is likely to increase demand among companies. Also valuable are surveys of business users - hearing directly from the would-be customers about why they are or are not adopting broadband, and how subscribers are using high-speed access.

Improving Security and Protecting Privacy: These are critic al to build and maintain consumer confidence, but they also represent a great opportunity. The security imperative will provide a strong catalyst for companies to re-engineer and re-think their entire operations. Successful business leaders will embrace new architectures and business processes that strengthen their place in the market and generate even greater productivity and efficiency through the use of technology. The security challenge will prove an opportunity for business. The Internet Security Alliance and Partnership for Critical Infrastructure Protection offer two good examples of industry- led efforts, although greater coordination is still needed.

Expanding Partnerships Among Educators and Researchers: The Internet2 is truly pioneering applications, services and models for online partnerships that will generate greater demand for higher-speed networks and ensure greater returns for those who use them.

Encouraging and Supporting Telework: Organizations such as the Telework Consortium are developing pilot projects to address telecommuting issues, identify and remove barriers and pioneer best practices. Likewise, businesses seeking greater broadband deployment can lead by example and promote telecommuting among their own employees.

Technology innovation will prove the greatest driver of broadband demand. New applications and services that consumers want and businesses need will provide the tipping point for broadband demand and usage. The developments that appear most likely to stimulate broadband demand include:

Developing DRM Solutions: Finding technical solutions to copyright challenges will expand digital content willing to go online, especially entertainment, and increase the value proposition for subscribers.

Improving Usability and Reliability of Broadband Equipment and Service: Making the broadband experience more plug-and-play - reducing deployment hassles and improving consumers' experience with service delivery - will increase demand for broadband and new broadband services.

Developing New Delivery Platforms: Consumers and businesses may be more interested in broadband over platforms that compete with cable and wireline platforms - such as wireless, satellite, optical fiber and perhaps eve n powerline. Such cross-platform competition would increase consumer offerings, keep prices low and encourage greater broadband adoption.

Improving Compression and Capacity of Existing Platforms: New technologies that deliver more data, more quickly over existing copper and coaxial infrastructures, such as the new MPEG 4 standard, will give consumers the broadband experience over existing and deployed infrastructure. As the surveys show, broadband usage is "sticky," and once consumers gain access to these applications they'll want more bandwidth.

Developing Alternative Deployment Techniques: New ways of deploying new lines, such as sewer access robots that deploy fiber without tearing up streets and at far less cost, or last mile wireless solutions, promise readier broadband availability and greater likelihood of adoption.

Broadband demand will grow as attack and solve many of the issues hindering quality of service in e-commerce—guaranteeing data rates, authenticating users quickly and securely, paying for goods and services without delay or burdensome forms, and transmitting reliable voice over IP over public networks.

3

Financial Management in a Networked World

Traditionally, Internet has treated all packets equally, and charging has involved only a fixed monthly fee for the access link to the network. However, there are signs of an imminent change. There is extensive work on provision of Quality of Service (QoS), with some transmissions getting preferential treatment.

Differential service will likely require more complicated pricing schemes, which will introduce yet more complexity. The motivation behind the work on QoS is the expectation of continued or worsening congestion. Overengineering has been traditional in corporate networks. Yet much of the demand for QoS is coming from corporations. It appears to be based on the expectation that overengineering will not be feasible in the future. The abandonment of the simple traditional model of the Internet would be a vindication for many serious scholars who have long argued that usage-sensitive pricing schemes and differential service would provide for more efficient allocation of resources.

The need for usage-sensitive pricing has seemed obvious to many on the general grounds of "tragedy of the commons". As Gary Becker, a prominent economist, said recently: An iron law of economics states that demand always expands beyond the supply of free goods to cause congestion and queues. It may indeed be an iron law of economics that demand for free goods will always expand to exceed supply.

An iron law of astrophysics states that the Sun will become a red giant and expand to incinerate the Earth, but we do not worry much about that event. Furthermore, the law of astrophysics is much better grounded in both observation and theoretical modelling than the law of economics.

In data networks, at first sight there does appear to be extensive evidence for that "iron law of economics." Comprehensive statistics are not available, but it appears that Internet traffic has been doubling each year for at least the last 15 years, with the exception of the two years of 1995 and 1996, when it appears to have grown by a factor of about 10 each year. Almost every data link that has ever been installed was saturated sooner or later, and usually it was sooner rather than later.

Based on current usage trends, this link will be saturated by the end of 1998, and will need to be upgraded, or else some rationing scheme will have to be imposed. To decide what is feasible or desirable, we have to consider the economics of the Internet.

The information they contain is often dated, and it usually covers only the Internet backbones. However, these backbones are a small part of the entire data networking universe.

The private line networks, in turn, are dwarfed by the LANs (local area networks) and academic and corporate campus networks. Most of the pricing and differentiated service schemes that are being considered, though, are aimed at Internet backbones or private line WAN links. Most of the effort on QoS schemes is based on the assumption of endemic congestion. However, when we examine the entire Internet, we find that most of it is uncongested.

That the LANs are lightly used has been common knowledge. However, it appears to be widely believed that long distance data links are heavily utilized. Even the backbone links are not used all that intensively, and the corporate private line networks are very lightly utilized. There are some key choke points (primarily the public exchange points, the NAPs and MAEs, and the international links) that are widely regarded as major contributors to poor Internet performance, but there is even some dispute about their significance.

Delays in delivery of email are frequent, but are almost always caused by mail server problems, as even trans-Atlantic messages do get through expeditiously. A large fraction of Web-surfing complaints are caused by server overloads or other problems. There are myriad other problems that arise, such as those concerned with DNS, firewalls, and route flapping.

Many QoS schemes require end-to-end coordination in the network, giving up on the stateless nature of the Internet, which has been one of its greatest strengths. Essentially all QoS schemes have the defect that they require extensive involvement by network managers to make them work.

However, it is already a major deficiency of the Internet that, instead of being the dumb network it is often portrayed as, it requires a huge number of network experts at the edges to make it work. Instead of throwing hardware and bandwidth at the problem, QoS would require scarce human resources.

Further, there are some obvious inefficiencies in the system that can be exploited. By moving away from private lines to VPNs (Virtual Private Networks) over the public Internet, one could provide excellent service for everybody through better use of aggregation of traffic and complementarity of usage patterns. The bulk of the work on QoS may be unnecessary.

QoS does have a role to play. There will always be local bottlenecks as well as emergency situations that will require special treatment. Even when local network and server resources are ample, there will often be need to ration access to scarce human resources, such as technical support personnel.

Even in the network, methods such as Fair Queueing can be valuable in dealing with local traffic anomalies, for example. Implementing them would represent a departure from the totally undifferentiated service model, but a mild one, and one that can be implemented inside the network, invisible to the users, and without requiring end-to-end coordination in the network.

Users in general behave sensibly, and although their demands for bandwidth are growing rapidly, these demands are reasonably regular and predictable. It appears likely that unit prices for transmission capacity will decline drastically, which should make it economically feasible to meet the growing demand. It is impossible to predict with any certainty how the Internet will evolve, especially since its evolution depends on many factors, not only basic computing and networking technology and possible appearance of the proverbial "next killer app," but also on government regulation and sociology.

The complexity of the entire Internet is already so great, that the greatest imperative should be to keep the system as simple as possible. The costs of implementing involved QoS or pricing schemes are large and should be avoided. One is the continuation of the current flat rate pricing structure with almost uniform best-effort treatment of all packets, and enough bandwidth to provide high quality transmission. That scenario is likely to materialize if transmission prices decline rapidly enough. If they don't, the second scenario might arise, still with flat rate pricing and undifferentiated service, but with pricing reflecting expected usage of a customer.

Finally, if even greater constraints are needed on traffic, ones that would provide congestion controls, approaches such as the Paris Metro Pricing (PMP) scheme of might have to be used. PMP is the least intrusive possible usage-sensitive pricing scheme possible, and my prediction is that if any usage-sensitive pricing is introduced, it will eventually evolve towards (or degenerate into) PMP. None of these three scenarios would meet the conventional standards for economic optimality.

The Internet (sometimes called the global Internet) refers to the entire collection of interconnected networks around the world that share a common addressing scheme. Further, U.S. usage, influenced by lower prices than in most of the world [ITU], foreshadows what the rest of the world will be doing within a few years, as prices are reduced. Data networks do not operate in isolation. To see them in the proper perspective, let us note that total spending on information technologies (IT) in the U.S. was about $600 billion in 1997, approximately 8% of gross domestic product.

The IT sector of the economy is credited with stimulating the high growth rate of the economy of the last few years, low unemployment, and low inflation [DOC]. Data communications cost about $80 billion in the U.S. in 1997, or 13% of total IT spending. In any event, today much more is being spent on voice phone services than on data. In the future, as broadband services grow, we can expect the balance to shift towards data. In particular, looking at total communications spending and how it is still dominated by voice, it is reasonable to expect substantial growth in spending on data transmission. The core of the Internet, namely the backbones and their access links, is surprisingly inexpensive.

There are many large estimates for total Internet spending, but those are misleading. There were about 20 million residential accounts with online services such as AOL at the end of 1997. At $20/month, they generated revenues of around $5 billion per year. However, most of that revenue is used to cover local access costs (the modems, customer service, and marketing expenses of the ISPs).

According to industry analysts [IDC], MCI's Internet revenues (which include only a small contribution from residential customers, and are dominated by corporate and regional ISP links to the MCI network) came to $251 million in 1997, and were running at an annual rate of $328 million in the last quarter of 1997.

Since MCI is estimated to carry between 20 and 30 percent of the backbone traffic, we can estimate total revenues from all backbone operations between $1.1 and $1.6 billion at an annual rate at the end of 1997. Compared to the Internet backbones, the total cost of private line networks is at least 6 times as large. Furthermore, the aggregate bandwidth of leased lines is also much greater than of the public backbones, although the traffic they carry appears to be comparable in volume. This helps explain why the evolution of the Internet is increasingly dominated by corporate networks. Just as with switched voice networks, data network costs are dominated by the local part. However, there is much more heterogeneity in data than in voice.

In the foreseeable future, large academic and corporate networks are likely to have 2.4 Kbps wireless links along with 14.4 and 28.8 Kbps modems, megabit xDSL and cable modem links, and gigabit fiber optic cables. In the local campus wired environment, overengineering with Ethernet, Fast Ethernet, Gigabit Ethernet, and similar tools appears certain to be the preferred solution.

However, there will still be challenges of interconnecting the other transmission components, as well as all the servers and other equipment that require the bandwidth. Network managers will have a hard time making everything interoperate satisfactorily even without worrying about QoS. The Internet backbones are small and inexpensive compared to the rest of the Internet. However, they are the heart of the Internet, just like a human heart that is small but crucial for the life of the body.

The role of the backbones will likely become even more important in the future as a result of several related developments. One is that they are being traversed by an increasing fraction of data traffic. The traditional 80/20 rule, which said that 80% of the traffic stayed inside a local or campus network is breaking down.

Ferguson and Huston even mention some networks where as much as 75% of the traffic goes over long distance links. Another reason for the increasingly important role of the Internet backbones is that they are supplanting private line networks as corporate WAN links, and with the development of extranets, will be playing a crucial role in the functioning of the whole economy. Thus there is a reason to worry about the costs of the backbones, as they might become a larger fraction of the total networking pie.

On the other hand, if one can overengineer only one part of the Internet, then it is best to do it to the core, as without high quality transmission at the core, other parts of the network will be only be able to offer poor service.

Network utilization rates are seldom discussed, yet they are the main factor determining costs of data services. A line that is used at 5% of capacity costs twice as much per byte of transmitted data as one whose average utilization rate is 10%. Although there is no simple relation between the quality perceived by customers and how heavily their networks are used, the less heavily loaded the network, the better the service.

Even the notoriously congested trans-Atlantic links do appear to provide good performance for applications as demanding as packet telephony in the early hours of Sunday morning. What this says is that even without any new QoS technologies, one can provide excellent quality by lowering utilization.

Thus the main problem of the Internet is not a technical one, but an economic one, whether one can afford to have lightly utilized networks. As an example, the experimental vBNS network, discussed in, provides quality sufficient for even the most demanding applications, but it is expensive, running at an average utilization of its links of around 3%.

For most people, an even more surprising feature of the data is the low utilization rate of private line networks. The reasons data networks are lightly utilized. Lumpy capacity is a major one. Rapid and unpredictable growth is another. Small private networks are yet another. Perhaps the main reason, though, is the bursty nature of data traffic. This traffic is bursty on both the short and long time scales, and customers do value such bursty transmission. This means that we cannot reasonably expect data networks to approach the efficiency with which the switched voice network uses transmission capacity. Utilization rates can also provide guides to the extent that QoS measures might improve perceived quality of networking.

Practically all Internet users find service much better in the morning than at noon. However, traffic on the backbones in the early hours of the morning is still about half that during the peak hours. Further, traffic mix does not seem to vary much between trough and peak periods.

Therefore we can conclude that during peak periods, no QoS measure is likely to provide transmissions that have priorities around the median of all traffic with better service than the current undifferentiated service provides for all traffic early in the morning. An important point in considering the low utilization rates of data networks is that it is not caused primarily by inefficiency or incompetence.

Customers choose the capacities of their lines, and their choices tell us what they want and what they are willing to pay for. Efficiency in utilization of transmission lines or switches should not be the main criterion for evaluating how good a network is. The crucial question is how well customers' needs are satisfied. The average utilizations were 52% at the University of Toronto and 78% at Columbia University. Clearly Columbia was utilizing its modems more efficiently.

Clearly much demand is unsatisfied, and there are many frustrated potential users who do not accomplish their work. Further, the high 78% utilization rate is misleading, since many users are probably staying online for longer periods than they would if they had assurance they could get a new connection when they wanted it.

For example, in the early days of computing, programs were written in assembly language. Later, as the industry advanced, there was a shift towards compiled programs. They typically run at half the speed of assembly coded versions, but they make software easier to write and more portable.

With further advances in computing power, industry was willing to jump on the Java bandwagon, even though the early versions of Java typically ran a hundred times slower than compiled programs. With over 99% of computing cycles devoted to running screen savers, this was a worthwhile tradeoff.

When capital costs are high, it makes sense to maximize the utilization of facilities. For example, latest semiconductor fab lines, approaching $2 billion in cost, are run around the clock. Among services that do face wildly varying demands, cannot stockpile their outputs, and have high fixed costs and lumpy facilities problems, the airlines manage to operate at 60-70% of capacity. They do this through intensive use of pricing. What is noteworthy about this example is that the yield management techniques used by the airlines are not liked by the public, but they work to keep the planes filled, while at the same time allowing people to fly at a moment's notice.

Airlines are an example of extremely expensive equipment that needs to be operated intensively. In contrast, LAN equipment is relatively inexpensive. Most of data traffic is on LANs, and it appears that utilization rates (measured over a week) are almost universally low, around 1%.

Users notice degradation in service when traffic grows, and respond by pressuring network administrators to increase capacity. In many organizations, LAN spending is controlled by small units, so that money not spent on LANs can be devoted to other purposes. When those units do overengineer, they must feel they are getting their money's worth.

Spending on LAN equipment is in the tens of billions of dollars, but that is only a fraction of the spending on PCs, say, and a tiny fraction of the salaries of the people relying on those LANs. Low utilization rates of LANs are a necessary penalty for good performance. The decisions on utilization rates of LANs are made in rather convoluted ways, with network administrators taking into account user complaints, plans for the future, available budgets, and other factors. Thus it is hard to say that the existing arrangement with 1% utilization factors is the outcome of a rational process.

Even though there was plenty of spare capacity on their phone lines (with average utilization of 4%), both households and businesses decided it was better to pay for additional lines than miss important calls, or bother switching between voice and fax. In earlier decades, similar considerations led to the effective elimination of party lines. In all these cases, individuals and businesses voted with their pocketbooks for lower utilizations and higher quality service. Although the connection is less clear than for phone lines, corporate Wide Area Networks (WANs) are lightly utilized because users either pay directly or else pressure their centralized networking organization for high quality data services.

Mission-critical applications cannot be neglected. What is important to realize is that data services customers decide on their utilization levels. Since they are paying for the higher bandwidth, we have to conclude that they do find it worthwhile. Almost all applications benefit from high bandwidth and low latency. Further, high bandwidth can often substitute for low latency, since, it is the transmit time of a whole file or screen image that needs to be minimized.

Since corporate IT organizations are always under pressure to cut costs, one might conclude that corporate LANs and WANs are properly provisioned for their tasks. If that is so, though, we are left with the puzzle of the Internet. Why does it not provide better service? As we have seen above, spending on the backbones of the Internet is a tiny fraction of the spending on LANs and WANs.

Diversion of a small portion of LAN and WAN budgets might seem to suffice to expand bandwidth of the backbones and solve the congestion problem. The solution to the Internet performance puzzle seems to have three parts. One is that given the utilization levels, lowering backbone congestion to that of a corporate WAN would involve about a 3 to 5-fold increase in capacity, with corresponding increases in costs.

Second is that the Internet lacks a method for users to signal providers effectively what quality of service they want and are willing to pay for. Third, most of the users of the public Internet are very price sensitive, and are (almost by definition, since they continuing to pay) comfortable with the present service. This is largely a legacy of the Internet's origins as an academic research network.

The public Internet is perfectly satisfactory for most applications, such as email. Even the notoriously congested trans-oceanic links do handle email expeditiously. Large database updates can also be handled, provided they can tolerate delays. It is only real-time applications, such as packet telephony, transaction processing, telnet, or video conferencing, and to a lesser extent Web surfing, that are negatively affected by congestion.

The Internet thus serves well what we might call the lower tier of the data networking market. On the other hand, corporate networks serve well the upper tier. What this means, though, is that they provide unnecessarily high quality of service for the lower tier demands. If a single level of service is all that can be provided, this is probably the optimal strategy for corporate networks.

Although packet networks are universally extolled as much more efficient than switched voice networks, they are surprisingly expensive. At most cor-porations, sending data over internal packet networks is more expensive than by using modems over the public circuit switched network. This is especially striking for two reasons. One is that modem calls use transmission capacity of the switched voice network extremely inefficiently.

Although 128 Kbps of network bandwidth is dedicated to each such call, usually only 28.8 or 33.6 Kbps worth of data is transmitted. The other reason is that only a small part (estimated by industry analysts at around $0.015 of the approximately $0.12 that the major carriers collect for a minute of a voice call in the continental U.S.) goes towards running their networks.

The cost of transporting a megabyte of data over a network is just one measure of performance, and it is seldom quoted. Customers usually do not pay per megabyte. However, the cost per MB is fundamental to understanding the economics of data networks. After all, the main function of these networks is to move bits from one point to another. Further, there is a clear distinction between transporting data overnight on magnetic tapes and sending it on a data network right away.

The distinction between transmission via a modem and the Internet is often immaterial to users. At the other end of the scale, the high value of reliable and low delay data communication is shown by the example of services such as Advantis, CompuServe, and Infonet, which as recently as 1993 were charging between $20 and $40 per MB.

This reinforces the claim made earlier that the Internet has grown not because of the low cost of packet data transmission, but because of the added functionality that such transmission made possible. The comparisons below involve apples, oranges, and pears. Further, all cost estimates are rough ones, due to lack of precise statistics. Still, it is worth looking at the numbers, especially since the disparities in costs are so large that they swamp any errors in estimates, and help explain the migration of data traffic from private lines to Frame Relay and the Internet.

Frame Relay is offered primarily in the form of PVCs (Permanent Virtual Circuits). There is a charge for a port, which imposes an absolute limit on the rate data can be sent into the Frame Relay network. There is also a charge for CIR (Committed Information Rate), which is the rate that the service provider guarantees to carry successfully to the destination. However, there is usually no charge for the amount of data transmitted.

Taking the total traffic carried for a variety of businesses, and dividing it into the prices paid for the service, it appears that on average Frame Relay providers collect revenues between $0.30 and $0.40 per MB. There are occasional references to a cost per MB of $0.03 or $0.05 for use of SVCs on Frame Relay or ATM networks. Although accurate, those figures are misleading, since they cover only the usage-sensitive component of the price.

With the low utilization levels that are observed, fixed costs dominate, and average $0.30 and $0.40 per MB. Private line costs per MB are even harder to estimate than those of Frame Relay. However, industry sources and reports in Data Communications and other magazines) report that Frame Relay is usually 20% to 50% cheaper than private line for equivalent service. (It is impossible to be precise, because this is an oranges-to-apples comparison. Among other factors, Frame Relay pricing does not depend on distance in the continental U.S., while that of private lines does.) This is confirmed by some sample data points, such as that of a large corporation in which network services are charged to departments according to their traffic, with total charges of $0.80 per MB.

There are several ways to do this. Residential customers currently stay connected about 45 minutes per day, according to public statements from AOL and other carriers, and while they are online, they transfer data at the rate of 5 Kbps. Thus they average 50 MB per month of data transfer, and at the standard rate of $20 per month, are in effect paying $0.40 per MB. The more interesting case is that of large business and academic customers who have dedicated high speed data lines to the Internet.

They usually pay for the local connection to the nearest Point of Presence (PoP) of their ISP, and then for the link to the ISP. The estimate of 3,000 TB per month of traffic on Internet backbones, together with the estimate of $1.5 billion per year for the revenue of those backbones yield an estimated cost of $0.04 per MB for the use of the backbones. This is almost an order of magnitude less than the cost of Frame Relay or private line transport.

As another confirmation that $0.04 per MB is a reasonable cost estimate for the Internet backbones, let us note that Web hosting services usually do have usage-sensitive pricing. For large data transfers, they typically charge between $0.03 and $0.05 per MB.

To be comparable to the current backbone providers, which pay for the links from their PoPs to their backbones, it seems reasonable to say that the total cost of the NSFNet backbone was around $18 million per year. Since this network carried about 6 TB per month in 1993, the cost per MB was $0.25.

Towards the end of 1994, traffic grew to 15 TB per month, but costs probably did not, so the cost per MB most likely dropped to $0.10 or so. The computations above suggest $0.04 per MB as the current cost of data transfer over the Internet backbones. However, that is not a full picture. Although comprehensive statistics are not available, it appears that the ISPs with national backbones (the NSPs) deal directly with only a small fraction of businesses that have Internet connections, primarily the big organizations with large capacity links.

Most of the small corporations go through regional ISPs. In terms of revenues, low bandwidth connections still dominate the private line market. Hence the cost of sending data for the bulk of business customers is likely to be considerably higher than the $0.04 per MB incurred by the typically larger customers that connect directly to the backbone providers. A crucial point in considering the costs of transporting data over various networks is that these costs are largely under user control.

Frame Relay, and Internet connection consist of fixed monthly charges, most users can save money by switching to lower bandwidth links. They have a choice, and by selecting the capacities and prices they do, they signal their interest in high quality transmission. However, the cost advantages of Frame Relay over private line networks, and of the public Internet over Frame Relay are widely accepted. For example, a study estimated annual costs of a small corporate network to be $133,272 using leased lines, $89,998 using Frame Relay, and $38,400 over the public Internet.

The major barrier to wide use of the public Internet by corporations is security, but that one is on the way to being overcome through the use of VPN (Virtual Private Networks). The other major barrier is performance. However, even there progress is taking place, with an increasing number of ISPs providing high quality transmission (within their networks) and even service guarantees.

The costs of data transfers over private line and Frame Relay networks are surprisingly high. Although packet networks are reputed to be extremely efficient, on average they cost more per MB than the switched voice network does. However, those costs are under customer control, in that it is the customers who decide how heavily to utilize their links, and therefore what their costs will be.

In the past, network managers coped with increased data traffic by moving to higher bandwidth links, which are much less expensive per unit of capacity. However, with growth rates in volume of data increasing, and leased line prices rising at an accelerating pace, it is natural that network managers are uncertain whether it will be possible to continue providing large pipes that are lightly utilized, and are asking for QoS measures to provide high quality transmission for at least the most important part of their traffic.

Although transmission prices have been rising, it seems likely that they will soon start decreasing. The main reason is that new technologies, primarily WDM

(Wavelength Division Multiplexing) are leading to dramatic cost reductions, and those will eventually show up in lower prices.

The greatest inefficiency in data networking today is that thousands of corporations are running their own private networks. Not only are the direct transmission costs higher than over the public Internet or the Frame Relay networks, but the indirect costs of network management are high as well.

A grave defect of the Internet is that in pushing intelligence to the edges of the network, it also pushed network administration and maintenance to the edges, where it is wastefully duplicated. Data traffic does not smooth out as much as voice traffic when it is aggregated. However, it does smooth out, and that is a part of the economic foundations for ISPs.

Estimates of traffic on the public Internet and on private line networks suggest that no single corporation carries even 1% of the total traffic. Even without smoothing gains, aggregation of traffic does offer huge savings. The reason is that price per unit of transmission capacity decreases dramatically as the bandwidth of a connection increases. These economies of scale reflect lower selling, administrative, and maintenance costs, as well as avoidance of many of the costs of the multiplexing hierarchy that is required to provide low bandwidth links on a fast fiber network.

A major reason for the high utilization of the long distance switched networks is that voice traffic can be predicted accurately and grows slowly. There is a large literature on teletraffic engineering that was developed over most of the 20-th century, and the prediction and traffic engineering tools that have been developed are surprisingly effective.

In studies of the economics of voice phone systems, there have been proposals for lowering costs by providing less capacity, so that many calls would be blocked during peak hours, and it would be the persistent callers, who kept redialing who would get through. However, this idea was never taken seriously. The switched voice system has attracted an enviable reputation for quality and usability by meeting even peak demands. Data traffic grows much faster than voice traffic, and is inherently much more bursty.

Such usage patterns have convinced many that data traffic is simply too chaotic to accommodate fully, and that rationing by queue will be essential for most traffic, with only a select portion getting high quality transmission using QoS tools. If even higher demand materializes, let some simple queuing mechanism take care of rationing access during the overload episode. If that is done, though, then on most days there will be no congestion at the servers, and no need for any complicated QoS mechanisms. If one had to build two separate networks for these two classes of customers, then, even ignoring the loss of efficiency coming from less aggregation, the total capacity of the two networks would have to be over 60% higher than that of the single network. Data traffic shows comparable differences in traffic patterns among different classes of users, differences that are similar to those observed in voice phone statistics.

Often natural demands are not sufficiently complementary to provide an even demand profile. In such cases, one can modify customer demands through pricing. In the Bell System, long distance rates depended on distance from the beginning. This pricing originated in the high marginal costs of setting up and carrying such calls.

On the other hand, prices were uniform around the clock until 1919. The network was largely idle in the evening and at night, yet it had to be kept operationa, since much of its value was in the ability to provide service at unusual times. It was sensible therefore to encourage use in off-peak hours through discounts.

There economic concerns were at the forefront of business planning, and an extensive literature was generated at the end of the 19th and in early 20th centuries. Interestingly, the literature on pricing of electricity was created primarily by engineers and businessmen, without noticeable input from economists.

Flat rate pricing for Internet access may turn out not to be sustainable, and the variations in traffic patterns among different classes of customers may not provide enough smoothing. In that case, it might be possible to use pricing to induce better utilization.

Pricing would not necessarily have to be usage-sensitive, in that one can have different prices for different classes of consumers, if one can discriminate among them, and prevent arbitrage. In the time-sharing arena, there have been successful examples of evening out the load through time-of-day pricing.

However, the rapid growth in processing power that has provided more cycles than people know what to do with, and this has put an end to just about the entire business of pricing processing power. It seems likely that in data transmission a similar phenomenon will apply.

QoS approaches would be of greatest value if networks were seriously congested, and the traffic requiring high quality transmission were a small fraction of the total. Under those conditions, creating an express lane for the priority traffic is sensible. However, neither of these conditions applies today, and it is questionable whether either will apply in the future.

Further, there are reasons to expect that prices of broadband transmission capacity will start a rapid and sustained decline, so that it will continue to be feasible to provide uncongested pipes. When utilization rates are low, users are clearly paying for the ability to burst at high speed. Many QoS schemes prioritize traffic depending on what application it comes from. This approach has many problems. Currently the majority of Internet traffic is http, and it is tempting to say that this represents "Web surfing" that should travel with lower priority than packetized voice, say.

However, much of this "Web surfing" may represent (in the future, if not now) customers making product inquiries or purchases, and it is questionable whether it should be consigned to a congested channel. In general, it is not at all clear whether high priority traffic will be a small fraction of the total.

Further, as IPSec and other encryption methods are applied to an increasing fraction of the traffic, it will be hard to decide based on packets alone what application originated them. Advocates of QoS appear not to have produced any quantitative analyses of the advantages of their schemes, nor of the costs of implementing them, although there are some admissions that those costs are not going to be negligible.

Most of the costs are likely to be hard to quantify ones, those involving application developers, end users, and especially network administrators. All those costs are already high. Many QoS schemes would require deployment throughout the Internet to be effective. That is a serious defect, given the tremendous heterogeneity and lack of centralized control, since there are plenty of ancient systems around, and no signs that changes will be any faster in the future.

Further, one of the most pressing issues for the future of the Internet appears to be that of ISP interconnections. It is already complicated, with no clear models as to what service agreements and settlements will be common. Throwing in QoS questions would only make this issue harder to resolve. In short, total system costs suggest that it would be best to confine most QoS measures to the edges of the network, for those infrequent cases where it is absolutely necessary.

The core of the network would be best run at a uniformly high standard for all traffic, with no end-to-end coordination. This would make it easier to reach and monitor agreements among customers and service providers, and would allow application developers and users a simple view of the network.

Some QoS methods could still be used in the core of the network, provided they were invisible to the end users. There are strong arguments for usage-sensitive pricing even in a network with a single class of service. Even in today's undifferentiated service model, there is a strong trend by corporate networks to charge business units according to their usage of the network, to promote greater awareness of costs and more rational use of resources.

Customers will have to have a clear incentive to send only the traffic that requires high quality service on the better channels. Pricing does not have to be onerous to have a large effect. Even a small charge can have a noticeable effect on human behaviour. In Internet access as well, small prices have often had large effects. For example, in Europe, residential Internet access is largely on a flat rate basis, but users have to pay the phone company for each minute of line use.

The result is a huge surge in Internet use in the evening, when the relatively modest per-minute phone charges drop. Although there are strong arguments for usage-sensitive pricing, the burden of introducing it would be heavy.

Careful accounting of traffic volumes would be required, as well as techniques for either sender or receiver paying. The switched voice phone system is often derided for its expensive billing system. However, that system is designed to be accurate, reliable, and auditable. Existing traffic monitoring schemes for packet networks are none of these things. When one examines current traffic statistics, there are many missing or clearly incorrect data points.

To introduce a robust usage-sensitive pricing mechanism would be a long and expensive undertaking. If there are to be per-byte charges on the Internet, they should be based on edge pricing; i.e., charging at the entrance and exit from the network, not based on what happens at internal nodes.

The simplest alternative to QoS is to simply provide the big pipes that will accommodate user demands, and continue to treat all packets equally as well as to charge fixed monthly fees only. As was shown earlier, this strategy would work with current networks and users.

Evidence shows that users would not go wild and instantly saturate the newly available bandwidth. Such networks would exploit the complementarity of traffic demands and the smoothing effect of aggregation of many sources to provide universally high quality transmission. This would minimize the cost to application developers, users, and network managers, and would let them concentrate on other serious issues.

There are reasons to expect that this strategy might work in the future as well, as prices of broadband capacity decline. However, it would be a race between demand and supply, and one could argue that the balance would be unstable, or else would settle into a situation like that of the current public Internet, where quality is mostly inadequate.

Backbone providers are beginning to levy extra charges on ISPs, and Web hosting services do have usage-sensitive pricing. When ISPs load their lines 10 times more heavily than corporate customers, the arbitrage opportunities and the disparities in costs imposed by different customers are just too large to ignore. Since these factors will continue in the future, it might be necessary to have a slightly more intrusive pricing scheme that does provide correct incentives for service providers and users.

Implications of Networks

Packet networks are growing explosively not because they utilize underlying transport capacity more efficiently, but because they provide much greater flexibility in offering new services. Study of utilization patterns shows there are large opportunities for increasing the efficiency of data transport and making the Internet less expensive and more useful. Utilization rates of networks have been strangely absent from most papers on the economics of the Internet, such as those in. However, these rates determine costs of services, since transmission links are priced by their maximal capacity.

Furthermore, utilization rates are the primary means by which network managers determine quality of transmission. Therefore it seemed important to consider current utilization rates on the Internet and the resulting costs. Such a study was carried out in. It uncovered a number of surprising results. For example, corporations in the U.S. spend more to transmit large files over their packet networks than they would if they used modems over the switched voice network.

The primary culprit behind this phenomenon is the low utilization of most data networks. A key point of the investigation of was the need to consider not just the public Internet, but the full universe of data networks and their role in the economy. For simplicity, only networks inside the U.S. were considered. Although they do attract intense attention, they are a small part of the entire IT (information technologies) industry.

While the IT sector of the U.S. economy accounts for about $600 billion per year [DOC], data communications costs about $80 billion, and of that, transmission comes to about $16 billion. Thus any modification to data networks has to be considered in light of the total costs it imposes on the economy, not just in terms of what it does to networks. Data networks are not only still a small part of the economy, they do not operate in isolation.

For voice calls, the basic service is easy to describe, and there is general agreement on desirable quality. On the other hand, data networks increasingly are becoming just enablers of other services, and few users care about the network by itself. What is important is how the entire application is perceived by the user, and network transmission is only a part of the system that makes that application possible. Even in the restricted realm of data networks, the public Internet is a small fraction of the total system.

Measuring networks by their maximal transmission capacity, it was estimated in that at the end of 1997 in the U.S., the switched voice network was probably still the largest, but the private line networks were about as large, and the public Internet was considerably smaller. Thus looking just at the public Internet does not give a proper perspective on data networks, especially since utilization patterns of private networks are considerably different. Although data networks are about as large as the voice network in bandwidth, the voice network still dominates in carried load, and is likely to do so for a few more years.

George Gilder's thesis is that bandwidth supply will soon be increasing so rapidly that we will not have to worry about network congestion. However, that argument is not entirely convincing. While technology will indeed increase supply, costs and prices are not the same in industries with high fixed costs, regulatory concerns, and substantial barriers to entry.

More important, while supply will be increasing, so will demand. Hence it is the balance between the two that will help determine the future of networks. Much of the "folk knowledge" about the Internet is simply false.

Packet networks are not necessarily more efficient than the switched voice network. Some of the new packet-only carriers have been showing comparisons in which IP transport saves more than 90% over the cost of traditional switched networks. In particular, savings on transport costs are widely perceived as the main advantages of carrying voice over packet networks.

On the other hand, when one considers existing networks, it turns out that most corporations spend more on transferring large files over their internal IP networks than they would if they used modems over the public switched voice network. This is an astounding result, since modems use only a small fraction of the bandwidth of the digital channel that is provided for voice calls. Further, network costs of voice calls are small compared to the prices charged.

There are thus unbeatable advantages to packet networks, but they are not in network costs, but in flexibility. The public Internet is small relative to other data networks. Although it is the public Internet that has caught all the attention, it is still dwarfed in transmission capacity and costs by the private line networks, as was shown in the tables in the Introduction. It is also far smaller than the switched voice network.

However, it is growing much faster, about 100% a year, than either the voice network, which is growing at around 10% per year, or the private line networks, which are growing at around 20-30% per year. Therefore in a few years the public Internet will be the dominant communication network, but it is not that yet. Few data networks are congested.

A surprising fact is that even though it provides high quality service, the switched voice network has considerably higher average utilization than any large collection of data networks. There is a general perception that the public Internet is hopelessly crowded, and even most network experts believe that private line networks are congested as well.

Some parts of the Internet are highly congested, especially the public peering points, the NAPs and MAEs. Many university links to the public Internet are also heavily loaded, which may have persuaded generations of students that all networks are heavily utilized. However, the backbones of the Internet are relatively lightly loaded.

It runs at a high fraction of its capacity for large parts of the day, but still manages to provide relatively high quality service, with minor delays and packet losses. Other ISP links show even higher utilization, frequent saturation, and high packet loss rates. While most corporate networks are run at low average utilizations, there are many exceptions.

Over a full week, average utilization might therefore be expected to be around 20%. Some international links have higher utilizations, over 30%. Congestion is not necessarily the biggest problem on the Internet. The "World Wide Wait" is often caused by problems other than lack of bandwidth.

A study carried out in 1997 by Christian Huitema about accessing some popular servers showed that 20% were not reachable. Among the 80% that could be reached, 42% of the delays were caused by network transmission, with DNS accounting for 13% and servers for the remaining 45%. Further, there are some indications that in the last couple of years, the performance of the backbones has improved, while servers are falling behind. If bandwidth were the critical resource in corporate networks, then surely it would be monitored closely.

Yet the study of utilization levels in was hampered by lack of data. Existing data was hard to obtain, since it is usually regarded as sensitive. In most cases, though, there was no data to release, since utilizations are not even measured consistently. Hence bandwidth is presumably just one of many problems that network managers have to deal with, and not necessarily the most important. In general, although the Internet is acclaimed as the simple network, it is extraordinarily complicated and hard to keep operational.

One of the major problems with the Internet is that most of the work of keeping it running has to be done at the edges, and so is wastefully duplicated, with network administrators at thousands of institutions doing essentially the same planning, implementation, and operational tasks. Often networks are not optimized because there are not enough skilled experts to do it. "The tragedy of the commons" may not be an insurmountable threat for the Internet. It is widely believed that queueing by congestion is the only way to run the Internet, since demand, driven by flat rate pricing, is insatiable.

There are many situations where adding capacity does not help. For example, road congestion in metropolitan areas can be relieved only temporarily by building more highways. The problem is that when travel speeds increase, people move further away, to take advantage of less expensive housing, opportunities to be closer to family, and other reasons.

However, in a dynamic environment with growing bandwidth, this argument is questionable. The "tragedy of the commons" argument is even suspect in slower growing industries. In data traffic, growth has been much faster than in telephone lines, and links have tended to get saturated. This is often cited as a prototypical "tragedy of the commons" problem.

Although the capacity of the link has had several sudden jumps, usage has grown at a pretty steady 100% a year. Thus these networks have not in general had to cope with sudden surges in demand that saturated new capacity as soon as it became available. Even when such surges materialized, they were contained by simple local measures. The orderly, although very rapid, growth in data traffic is probably caused by a combination of several factors.

Available content, user skills and awareness, and the network infrastructure all have to develop in parallel. The last factor is especially important. Users don't just go and exploit the Internet. Except for cases of malice, they usually need to have a substantial local infrastructure in order to make use of the wider networks, and this limits the growth in demand for connectivity.

The "bursty nature of data traffic" is not the culprit behind low utilization rates of data networks. Data traffic does not smooth out as well as switched voice traffic, and it shows long range dependence. However, that does not mean that high utilization cannot be achieved. Most of data transport uses TCP, which fills available bandwidth and can produce high load factors. High utilization thus had to come from explicit or implicit choices about the quality of data transport to be provided.

Economic efficiency means satisfying customers' demands. Engineering efficiency means providing a service with the minimal amount of resources. The two are often in conflict. The switched voice system provides a compromise that is more efficient than the Internet in both economic and engineering aspects. It gives a high quality service to its customers any time they want to use it, and yet manages to have a higher utilization rate of the transmission facilities.

There are basic reasons for low utilization rates of data networks that are caused by the rapid growth rate of data traffic and the economies of scale in purchases of transmission links. However, the main cause of this low utilization rate of private line networks is the attempt to satisfy user needs. Latency is the key issue. However, it is not packet latency, the concern of most of networking literature, that matters. It is transaction latency, the time it takes to complete whatever one cares about (transmitting an email message or downloading a Web page), that is important.

Transaction latency can be lowered to a large extent by going for higher bandwidth. Since most of the traffic on the Internet is HTTP, it is often dismissed as just Web-surfing. However, Web-surfing includes customers downloading product information or placing orders, as well as employees accessing corporate databases. Therefore it often deserves high priority.

However, Web-surfing does produce traffic patterns such as that of low average utilizations, when it meets user demands. An important feature of the quote above is that it did not refer to any quantitative measures of network performance. There are certainly studies of what performance is required for tasks such as transaction processing, and how different network technologies compare in satisfying those requirements.

The importance of the subjective factor in judging network performance is also apparent in the choices of circuit speeds. They are usually chosen in simple multiples of some basic rate even when intermediate speeds are available. The human perceptual system operates on a logarithmic scale, and therefore it requires large steps to achieve a noticeable improvement in performance. Low utilizations of data networks should not be surprising.

Comparisons of PCs never discuss how much they will be used, and instead concentrate on benchmarks showing how much time those PCs take to perform various tasks. What the resulting low utilizations mean is that the lightly utilized resource is inexpensive enough compared to the value people place on its availability and their time.

By moving to PCs we have lowered the utilization of the equipment, but have provided much more flexibility. On the other hand, the high utilizations of international links. When links are as expensive as they are now across the Pacific or the Atlantic, it appears that IT managers either implicitly or explicitly decide to make their users put up with congested networks. The high utilizations of ISPs links most likely reflect a combination of extreme price sensitivity of the residential modem customers and of the difficulty those customers would have in deriving any benefit from uncongested links.

The high latencies and low transmission speeds of modems would guarantee low quality experience in any event. The comparison of utilization rates of trans-oceanic and domestic corporate links suggests that if prices come down, users will opt for higher quality transmission and thereby lower utilizations. This is what appears to have happened in the LAN environment.

On the other hand, today LAN utilizations at the institutions that was able to obtain the data for (which is not many, and consist primarily of those places that use the MRTG tool [MRTG]), tend to be around 1%. Further, in those institutions that have both 10 Mbps and 100 Mbps Ethernets, the average utilizations of the 100 Mbps links tend to be around half or a third of the rate of 10 Mbps links.

LAN equipment has decreased drastically in price, and so it has become easier to satisfy people's desire for bursty transmission. It has also become less expensive to solve problems by tossing bandwidth at them instead of using scarce and expensive network manager time.

There is an attempt to economize, and connections get upgraded to 100 Mbps Ethernet only when there is a need for such speeds. In general, though, other pressing network problems are clearly more important than maximizing utilization of network bandwidth. The general conclusion about low utilization rates of corporate networks is that they are not a sign of waste, but of the value of high quality data communications and of the complexity of running networks.

Utilization rates and utilization patterns may explain why some technologies have flourished and others have fallen by the wayside. During the 1980s, there was a serious competition between Ethernet and Token Ring technologies for the LAN market. One of the claimed advantages of Token Ring was supposed to be its ability to carry a higher fraction of its peak capacity in routine operations.

Another advantage was that Token Ring had QoS support built in. The technical and economic issues were complex, but the primary reason it lost out appears to be that it was more complicated. Similarly, it appears that ATM has failed to take off largely because it is inappropriate for most of today's networks.

ATM was conceived with the idea, inspired by voice and multimedia, that traffic would consist of long-lived flows with reasonably well defined bandwidth, latency, and jitter requirements. However, that is not what we have on our networks today. Most of the traffic consists of Web page downloads that are small, and what matters is how quickly the entire page is delivered.

Therefore ATM is irrelevant from users' perspective. It finds its greatest applications in core networks, where aggregate traffic flows do resemble the traffic conditions for which ATM was designed. Most QoS measures are also of doubtful utility in the current environment.

Both ATM and QoS might become much more relevant if the Internet changes. ATM already plays a big role in the core of the network, as the basic transport mechanism used by the backbones to carry IP traffic. The focus here is on how the Internet appears to the users and system administrators at the edges of the network, and from their point of view ATM does not offer serious advantages, and does have serious shortcomings.

Further, techniques such as Weighted Fair Queueing (WFQ) and Random Early Detection (RED) can be invaluable in controlling congestion, and can be implemented inside the network without destroying the exceedingly valuable stateless nature of the Internet, and without complicating the lives of users or even the lives of users' system administrators. Such simple techniques might suffice to provide congestion controls for networks that offer uniformly high quality of service to all traffic.

Some congestion responsive techniques are essential. Even the highest priority transmissions will occasionally have to compete for limited bandwidth with other transmission of similar priority. Therefore essentially all applications will have to possess some mechanism for limiting their bandwidth demands in the presence of congestion.

Since the human perceptual system is insensitive to small changes, very simple, although suboptimal, algorithms like the ones in TCP, WFQ, and RED should suffice, especially if the network is not heavily loaded. The Internet community appears to be learning precisely the wrong lessons from the switched voice networks.

The ideas that data moves in flows and that precise guarantees of service quality are required appear to be inappropriate for the Internet, and are leading to development efforts that are likely to be of little use. On the other hand, there are valuable lessons that can be learned from the traditional phone networks. One of them is simplicity. The Internet is just too complicated.

A telling sign is that only about two thirds of U.S. households that have PCs also have Internet accounts. In contrast, the phone system has developed simple user interfaces and standards that allow billions of people to use it easily.

There is an unavoidable conflict between simplicity and flexibility, and the phone system is not flexible enough to survive in its present form. On the other hand, the Internet will surely have to become simpler to attract more users. Furthermore, there should be ways to do that without sacrificing much flexibility, by moving towards standards such as IPv6, providing more security inside the network, and so on. Another important lesson that the Internet can learn from the switched voice network is about economics. It is worth remembering that initially the phone was an extremely expensive technology.

A hundred years ago, monthly charges for phone service in New York City amounted to half of the average monthly wage. Yet with diligent effort, phone service has become affordable for the masses. Some factors that went into the high utilization of the switched voice network are the slow and predictable rate of growth of voice traffic, factors that do not apply to the Internet.

However, there are other factors that can also be taken advantage of in data networks, such as complementary traffic patterns and statistical aggregation. Yet in data networks, we have corporate private line networks that are used mostly just during the business day. We also have ISP networks used primarily by residential customers, who use them largely in the evenings and on weekends for graphs of usage patterns. Those networks are disjoint. If they were combined, they could provide a uniformly high quality of service to all current traffic at all times and do so with lower total capacity than the separated networks have now.

Aggregation of traffic is another great opportunity for the Internet. If data networks were as congested as is widely believed there would be little that could be done. However, corporate users purchase lines for their burst capacity, so utilizations are low, and the situation is vastly different. Furthermore, this would still be corporate traffic only, which is significant only during the regular business day. By mixing in the complementary household traffic patterns, it might be possible to raise utilization levels by factors of four compared to the current levels, and provide uniformly high quality service for all traffic.

A large common network would also serve to reduce the enormous administrative costs of running separate corporate networks with point-to-point connections. It might also make it easier to provide some form of the dynamic routing that has been so important in reducing costs and increasing utilization rates in switched networks.

In general, the cost advantages of a single common network have been demonstrated overwhelmingly with electric and other utilities, but are still waiting to be realized in data networks. The costs advantages of a large common data network are already being partially realized by the Internet backbones.

However, to be a convincing substitute for private line networks, the public Internet will have to provide higher quality and security. Quality on many backbones already appears to be sufficient, and VPN (virtual private network) technology exists to assure necessary security. The main objection to QoS is that it would complicate the Internet.

As a simple example, if traffic priority were to be set according to application, then either encryption technologies such as IPSec, which conceal packet payloads, would have to be banned, or else an elaborate additional signalling scheme would be required.

The ideal solution is to keep the Internet as close to a dumb network as possible, one that just accepts packets and delivers then to the destination. As in the switched voice network, this might require building in more intelligence inside the network (to deal with security issues, for example), but it should be intelligence that is invisible to the end users.

Although the ideal of a simple network is very attractive, there are advantages to more complicated systems. In particular, several levels of service quality would lead to more efficient use of network capacity. Today, all corporate traffic, including delay-insensitive file transfers, receive the same high quality service, and in addition, networks are idle most of the time. On the other hand, on the public Internet, there are choke points that lead to frustration with the "World Wide Wait," yet there is no way for users to obtain better service.

A network offering different levels of service to different types of traffic therefore has attractions. All the standard economic arguments argue in favour of such a solution. Charges do not have to be high to have a noticeable effect on human behaviour.

Any universal differential service scheme will almost inevitably involve a usage sensitive pricing system. So far such pricing has been applied only in limited cases, most notably in countries such as Chile, New Zealand, and Australia, where communication costs to the U.S. are very high. However, with traffic increasing and transmission costs still growing, charging per byte is spreading.

Even corporate IT managers are implementing it, in order to allocate costs to divisions. So far, though, all such charges are simply for each byte sent or received.

This has obvious attractions all by itself, as it would promote fairness. As it is, flat rate pricing means that corporations that use their Internet links lightly pay the same as ISPs and universities that transmit at high fractions of the capacity of their connections. This is already leading to modifications of the standard flat rate approach, with ISPs often facing higher charges than other users.

Even with simple per-byte charging, there are problems caused by the lack of a reliable measurement infrastructure. With differential services, the accounting difficulties increase. Traffic counts would have to become more robust, and there would surely have to be a substantial infrastructure to allow either the sender or the receiver to pay.

Users would be free to select for each packet which channel to send it on. The expectation is that the more expensive channels would attract less traffic, and therefore would be much less congested. The details of PMP and in particular further justifications for it are contained in. The basic intuition of PMP is to have a scheme that is as simple as possible. If there are going to be different service levels on the Internet, there will have to be differential pricing.

We are entering a new era, with new technologies and new competitors. Until recently the Internet was so small, that even its 100% per year growth rate did not affect the much smaller growth rate of the underlying telecommunications network.

Very soon, though, that growth rate for the Internet will mean a similar growth rate for the entire network, which is likely to lead to rapid introduction of new equipment and a rapid decline in prices. Unfortunately, it is impossible to predict how soon transmission prices will start declining.

ATM and many QoS schemes were dismissed in an earlier section as irrelevant for today's Internet on the grounds that current traffic does not consist of extended flows with well-defined rate requirements. However, the Internet can change extremely rapidly. After all, hardly anyone had heard of the Web half a dozen years ago, and yet it is now the dominant application on the Internet.

4

Managing Information Security

Since the early 1990's with the advent of the Internet and the networked economy security has shifted from a single point or even point to point issue. Business is now conducted increasingly over intranets and extranets, across virtual private networks, via remote access over the Internet and is increasingly engaged in via wireless gateways. These online, remote interactions accommodate one to one, one to many and many to one interactions. New technologies and business models have developed to accommodate this migration to online commerce, at the business-to-business, business to government and business to consumer levels. When the OECD last reviewed the Guidelines, security issues were much more straightforward involving fewer parties and less complexity. The open and interconnected nature of systems today creates a different context within which to analyze these issues and review the Guidelines. Two evolving and interrelated spheres of expertise and responsibility should be noted at the outset. The first is the sphere of economic security. The second concerns the interconnected spheres of the local, national, regional and global critical infrastructures.

The latter go beyond communications networks to include power grids and the other essential infrastructure services upon which economies and societies depend. As companies have become more dependent on online communications and technology for data storage management, and interchange, the security of these systems has become a paramount business imperative. While neither sphere is the exclusive purview of either government or industry, each has a natural dominant player. Critical infrastructure has been the historic domain of governments, but in today's information technology field it is inherently the province of business and government cooperation. Business and government must and do engage in close cooperation and consultation on these issues but the final decision and implementation responsibility rests with governments. In the economic security sphere, business is the only actor that can make final decisions on what solutions are appropriate to deploy to protect a variety of systems that provide a variety of services and functions.

Business is and has been cooperating across industries and geographies with business, government and users/consumers to help determine what needs must be met and how best to meet them. Clearly, business has taken the lead in this area through innovation, competition and the ability to deploy products in a global marketplace. The shift from government to industry in this sphere of information security cannot be understated. In fact, given the historic shift away from the Cold War environment, coupled with the increasingly global nature of business, the use and export of security technology has been progressively deregulated around the world. With the advent of the web browser in 1993 and the commercialisation of the Internet, security technology began to be widely available around the world, often via download or bundled with a new PC or device as part of network access or with some form of computing power. It is important to recognize that information security is not just about encryption software or hardware. Services from consultants and e-services provided by websites, hosting services, application service providers (ASPs), online exchanges, and e-marketplaces, all touch information security in many significant ways. Corporate networks, government networks, and university networks, both old and new, also significantly impact information security given the magnitude of information stored on them and transmitted over them.

Information sharing is an essential element in security. At present there are many partnership activities focused on information sharing and analysis, awareness building, and cooperation. Recognizing the fact that industry, in most cases, has capitalized, designed and built the information infrastructure, industry must continue to lead in protecting its assets and using them responsibly. Solutions need to be appropriate to the problems and must be developed in cognizance of the most recent hazards and technologies. Bureaucratic processes are not appropriate for such varied and real time solution development and deployment needs. In order to ensure effective security, all owners and operators of networks need to have a better understanding of the activities that take place on their networks. Information security practices and technology are becoming increasingly sophisticated in order to fulfill this need for management visibility into the network. One can try to put more walls up to protect their digital assets. Connecting one's network to other networks is, however, an increasing fact of life. Moreover, threats to security may come from both inside the organization and external sources.

Management in both industry and government need to know on a real time, ongoing basis, whether the actual traffic on their network conforms to their expectations. Institutions in the private and public sectors all have rules governing the conduct of their employees, vendors, and customers, especially with regard to property, contracts, and sensitive information. Today, institutions old and new are applying rules, business practices and policies to their networks so that they can effectively measure the traffic flowing over them. For instance, unusually heavy traffic may be an indication of an attack. These statistics must, however, take into account certain anomalies or periodic disruptions of traffic flow. One cannot manage what one neither measures nor understands. This may seem obvious but it is an important point to make at the outset—any attempt to completely divide the world of information security into an industry zone and a government zone is antithetical to the inter-networked culture of modern computer driven communications. And, while there may be dominant spheres of influence, collaboration on many levels will be required.

Collaboration between government and industry, though essential can raise legitimate business concerns relating to new forms of liability and costs for supporting law enforcement activity. Likewise governments are trying to find resources to keep pace with the technology and expertise of 'threat sources'. Balancing these interests in the collaboration process will be essential.

There is a common interest between industry and governments to ensure a sound and safe environment in which to do business. Without such a safe environment economic security of both is at risk. When an institution does not manage its information assets properly, its partners or customers may lose trust in the institution; this applies to both public and private sector institutions.

The words 'security' and 'privacy' and 'reliability' mean different things to different people in different contexts. In this rapidly changing environment, it is impossible for anyone to guarantee in a contract that any product, high technology or otherwise, is totally secure. The Information Security Guidelines will benefit from the addition of a glossary of terms and definitions. This glossary might help set expectations of meaning and build awareness and consensus, but will define the scope and intent of the terms as used in the Guidelines themselves. This matter deals with information security in terms of several discrete topics that are of critical importance. The topics of this outline include the following: prevention; voluntary private sector initiatives; relevant technology standards; terms and definitions; user interests; cooperation among international and regional organizations; the role of government; survey information on threats; survey information on vulnerabilities.

Public-private partnerships such as the Information Sharing and Analysis Centers (ISACs) in the US are a step toward enabling prevention and evidence of industry's historical role in prevention. A fundamental element of prevention is that security is enhanced through knowledge Industry has led this growth in prevention capacity and capability; industry needs to continue its work with the recognition and support of governments around the world. Information sharing and analysis has long been a part of the culture of the information security professional community.

From the dynamic of competing to test and defeat one's own systems so that they can be strengthened and improved, to the collaborative nature of computer professionals in academic and corporate environments, sharing information about bugs, threats, vulnerabilities, upgrades, implementation, and coding itself is endemic to the collaborative nature of the Internet. For years companies have run their own security teams that identify problems, create fixes and distribute patches to customers. These practices are evolving and developing rapidly as companies better understand and anticipate the threats posed by online criminals. In addition, information sharing and analysis websites, list-serves, email alerts, and other services have grown up around the increasing need to deal with information security.

From the Computer Emergency Response Team (CERT) that originated out of Carnegie-Mellon University, to privately run websites such as SecurityFocus or Bugtraq, industry and its professional experts use the medium to collaborate in real time about the latest security threat. Viruses, for example, are so common now that many information security professionals are usually able to find fixes or other remedies within minutes, hours or a day. Such rapid response results, in part, from the open nature of the industry collaboration. Originally, CERT's work was almost exclusively incident response (IR).

Since then, CERT has worked to help start other incident response teams, coordinate the efforts of teams when responding to large-scale incidents, provide training to incident response professionals, and research the causes of security vulnerabilities, prevention of vulnerabilities, system security improvement, and survivability of large-scale networks. CERT is funded primarily by the US Department of Defense and a number of Federal civil agencies, but it also receives an increasing amount of private sector funding as well.

The other private sector security organisations (PSSOs) such as SecurityFocus are relatively new organizations. SecurityFocus actually manages Bugtraq, a vulnerability mail list, which has been around for quite some time. Other PSSOs such as SecurityWatch are too new to evaluate effectively but demonstrate the pro-activity of the private sector.

These PSSOs and others supplement the work occurring within technology companies to analyze their own products, to create fixes where necessary, to publish and distribute patches, and to incorporate their learning into new product development. Moreover, technology companies regularly collaborate informally to share information about potential threats. Most organizations of this type perform very helpful functions for the information security community. They distribute the latest information on vulnerabilities of all kinds (worms, viruses, operating system and protocol vulnerabilities, automated scripts, etc.) and provide incident response advice and assistance (especially CERT). They are an important resource for the timeliness and comprehensiveness of the information they provide. It is important to recognize that government has tolerated, recognized and benefited from industry leadership in this area, and industry has moved to formalize some of these community and private activities, such as creating ISACs for individual sectors, as mentioned above. Some individuals in the Internet community may not immediately understand or agree with such formalization, which seems inconsistent with the decentralized nature of the Internet.

However, informal, ad hoc contributions to the Internet community will not stop, despite the creation of these formal activities. Experts from academia, government and the private sector will continue to try to find security vulnerabilities and solve them. Also, given the self interest companies have in maintaining and increasing the confidence consumers have in using the Internet, businesses will continue to drive improvements to information security. Auditing of one's network operations and information security practices is critical to the real prevention of harm and to defeat security problems.

The Global Business Dialogue for Electronic Commerce (GBDe) recommends that 'governments and companies should invest in information assurance and cyber security products, services, and procedures to protect the value of their business, and government information and content, and to prevent misuse by cyber criminals. All stakeholders must ensure that users can safely do business on the Internet. Knowing more about the behavior of the traffic running through one's network enables the improvement of network health and security. Companies need to be in better control of the traffic and what happens to it while it is on their network. Rather than merely reacting to threats or vulnerabilities, many businesses are actively monitoring activity on their networks, and any anomalous traffic is immediately detected and dealt with in real time. This proactive approach is very effective and efficient; it can also detect non-security aspects such as general performance and support network diagnostic awareness.

The technical deployment and implementation of systems and networks are within the normal purview of information systems professionals. The responsibility for security, however, needs to be considered at the corporate officer and Board level in the private sector and at the ministerial level in Governments. Policies and practices related to information security must be understood at those levels for ministers of government departments and CEOs of private companies to raise awareness of and support efforts aimed at the prevention of harm to their respective networks. Increasingly the network has become the core asset of their respective enterprises. If this is not done, both businesses and governments risk liability, loss of productivity, a decrease in user confidence, and increased costs of doing business. Security is in fact a tool for productivity, efficiency and reliability. A proactive, rather than a reactive approach, is necessary and is starting to evolve. Prevention is also closely linked to further liberalization of security technologies. Given the decentralized and open nature of the Internet, export and import controls remain as barriers to security. Continued progress toward liberalization will enable systems to be further strengthened against attacks by bad actors with or without the same technology. Industry and government need to continue to work together on addressing the ongoing challenges created by the Internet. Given the borderless nature of the Internet, attempts by governments to assert control may undermine prevention and security.

Voluntary private sector initiatives drive improvement in the area of information security. Sometimes referred to as codes of conduct, such tools are and should be developed by the private sector. There can be no single code of conduct appropriate to the broad circumstances and context of security. To attempt such drafting would remove the flexibility essential to e-business and the necessary tailoring and context-specific development and implementation of security solutions.

While some have argued for the establishment of a single, global e-security organization (e.g., the World E-Commerce Forum), many in government and industry oppose such an idea. The World E-Commerce Forum was prompted by the OECD, UN (Committee for International Trade Law), WTO and WIPO in 1998 to create a Forum with the following objectives: 'To provide a means of communicating initiatives being taken at the global inter-governmental level to the e-commerce strategists and policy makers they most effect, and to provide a Forum where those global e-strategists can share their techniques and practices.' However, the Forum's own panel of experts (four government, one industry) argued strongly against it. The debate among the panel of experts revealed that there is already a tight and highly effective network of national government security agencies working together to combat cyber-crime. Industry and government already cooperate in various ways on education and training. Given the pace of technical change law enforcement and government rely to some extent on the expertise of industry leaders.

Voluntary industry initiatives have been and will continue to develop from experience and will be context driven. They cannot be mandated in a top down approach through government regulation or liability rules established through jurisprudence. Given the fast pace at which the character of networks and technology change, legislated codes of conduct simply cannot keep up. A one-size-fits-all approach would be difficult to achieve in the global and decentralized Internet. Also, each industry sector best understands its security needs and its customers' needs.

Since those sectors cross national and regional borders, they will be, and are, more likely to drive harmonization and arrive at a common basis for private sector initiatives. Moreover, the Internet's decentralized and non-commercial open roots do not lend itself to top down, central approach to rule-making, where a single body promulgates mandatory rules or guidelines for information security. It is highly unlikely that such an approach would ever be accepted, function as desired, or add value in terms of trust and confidence. Also, owners and operators of networks know what their networks do and how they do it, including managing their network's relationship with other networks. Contract law, operations driven by private sector developed technical standards, competition, and customer demand are driving best practices. Finally, it is important to recognize that voluntary cooperative initiatives by industry may implicate antitrust, government information disclosure and liability issues. Specifically collaborative rules or government regulations authorizing such cooperative security arrangements may compel disclosure of proprietary or otherwise sensitive information to the government, the public or a private entity. Such collaboration may also enable anti-competitive behavior. The information shared may need to remain private and otherwise protected. If companies abide by publicly stated practice, how is their liability to their customers and others impacted? Liability is an issue that should be left to negotiations among the contracting parties. If the risk of liability is too great the initiative will not succeed.

The rapid growth of e-commerce has been achieved through the development of flexible private-sector standards for technology and services. Given the changes since 1992, industry, government and users should commit themselves to a technology environment in which standards are developed by industry through a voluntary, industry led, market-driven standards process, relying, where present on accredited, authoritative national and multinational standards bodies. The private sector is best suited for this role because it is the prime developer of security products and can respond more quickly through more streamlined mechanisms. Indeed, the private sector is leading this work through the development of international expert groups and standards mechanisms. If governments choose to participate in the standards process it should be as a user and procurer of commercially available technology. Notwithstanding the diversity of approaches to standards setting and recognizing the cultural differences between national and regional markets, information security will suffer under regimes that favour government led or mandatory preferences. Such standards are not likely to be customer driven and more likely to be tailored toward supporting a division or markets or an accommodation of a proprietary or legacy technology or business model.

Information security improves only as technologies and systems are proven to be weak or as they are in fact broken;. government mandated standards may thwart such natural improvement and debilitate security. Technical standards range from specific implementation for encryption algorithms in software to broad and complex information technology infrastructures to specification of entire system architectures. They also touch business methods and processes as well as web based e-services. There are many technical standards efforts shaping information security.

There are at least three groupings of user interests. First, consumer and individual liberty advocacy groups such as the Center for Democracy and Technology (CDT), the Electronic Privacy Information Center (EPIC) and the Global Internet Liberty Campaign (GILC), provide useful substantive information. Second are those commercial firms who depend on their customers and as a result purport to speak on their behalf. Large Internet media and communications firms as well as software and hardware companies come to mind. Also, there are new business models such as those utilizing peer-to-peer technologies and architectures that also have a large community of individual users and may be able to provide a unique view of user interest. Finally, there are the views of business users. Vendors that deal with business users every day can readily describe what information security issues are of interest to their users. For now we include government networks as users in this group insofar as they too procure and use information security technology. However, their interests are likely to diverge when it comes to issues of national security and law enforcement matters— subjects beyond the scope of this analysis.

Role of international and regional organizations

There is a strong need to work in parallel and in cooperation across international and regional organizations. Whether it is the Council of Europe CyberCrime Treaty process, the European Commission, legislation and regulation at the national level from countries such as the US (e.g., National Information Protection Commission) and UK (e.g., Carnivore, Regulation of Investigatory Powers (RIP)), G8 work on CyberCrime, or Interpol, government organizations at various levels are engaged. Also, various business and technical organizations are involved: Global Business Dialogue for Electronic Commerce (GBDe); Global Internet Project (GIP); Information Technology Association of America (ITAA) and the World Information Technology and Services Alliance (WITSA) Global Information Security Summits and broad IT sector Information Security Committee work; Internet Societal Task Force (ISTF); World Wide Web Consortium (W3C); Internet Society (ISOC); and the International Chamber of Commerce (ICC) and its CyberCrime Task Force. There are also public-private efforts: InfraGuard and Internet Technology Security Group (ITSG) from the US FBI with participation from industry, academia and individuals; Computer Emergency Response Team (CERT), the NSTAC, NSIEs, and the NCC partnership between Government and industry.

Government as a consumer of information technologies can help to improve information security in a very significant way. Government agencies and ministries use information security technologies, products and services. E-government is a growing topic of discussion among industry and government. From online voting, to payment of taxes, to driver's license registration, to many other government services, government should first and foremost focus on improving its information security. Government has to improve, as it has to upgrade its own information technology systems in order to deliver services to its constituents and to make its own employees more productive.

Once more as international, regional, national, and sub national governments begin this process they will be better prepared to participate in the public policy discussions regarding information security. Each day industry contends with the challenges of information security and government networks also wrestle with similar challenges. Government should approach information security from the perspective of a user. Practical, first hand experience will give government a better understanding of the market incentives that drive industry to create its ever-superior security products and services. The role of government may become one of the most widely discussed topics in the review and revision of the OECD Guidelines. At this relatively early stage in the 'Internet era' review of the Guidelines, the Global Internet Project (GIP) has recommended that governments should not dictate characteristics, such as levels of security or impose standards.

GIP instead asks that governments collaborate with the private sector to: increase cooperation and information sharing; lead by example with adoption of security approaches in their own computer systems and services to constituents and employees; energetically investigate computer crime and prosecute computer criminals; promote the use of open voluntary, industry led standards; remove the remaining controls on civilian encryption technologies; provide more details from their threats and vulnerabilities assessments, perhaps in a non-classified form; support pre-competitive research on security (e.g., research and development in the area of quantum physics and cryptography) and technical collaboration in the area of application development and math and science education; fund the education and training of information security experts to help bridge the every present skills gap (i.e., need to consider the need to drive down the cost of security by increasing supply of expertise as well as improving the competitiveness by increasing the number of participants and perspectives); and encourage and support efforts by the private sector to teach children and teenagers how to behave ethically in a virtual world (e.g., the Information Technology Association of America (ITAA) has begun work in this area). Perhaps the most comprehensive work in this area describing the role of government is the informative work by the Global Business Dialogue for Electronic Commerce (GBDe). The GBDe's CyberSecurity and CyberCrime white paper published September 2000 spells out recommendations for industry and government action.

Some action is to be shared; other actions are to be left to each side alone. Areas of collaboration between government and industry include: global cooperation to deal with cybercrime; investment in information assurance services; use of existing cybersecurity tools and the development of new tools; research and development funding; cyberethics; state-sponsored industrial espionage; mutual cooperation with law enforcement where appropriate. GBDe recommends that government act to: frame international agreements to combat cybercrime; clarify substantive criminal laws; not increase regulatory control; avoid shifting costs to industry; carefully consider the use of government owned investigative technology; remove controls on encryption; encourage the development of industry-led standards to protect proprietary information and content; continue government-to-government coordination and cooperation at the international level; and address the shortage of skilled workers.

All parties, government and industry alike, must be cognizant that the market for security products and services is dynamic, innovative and growing with great speed. Government intrusion will stop this growth through burdensome, unintended consequences that stifle business and needlessly limit personal freedoms. These burdens may be in the form of actual regulatory compliance obligations or may be the result of reporting or other administrative requirements. Lastly, these burdens are not always readily apparent to policy makers in terms of sheer volume, potential overhead and compliance costs. Recognizing and minimizing these potential burdens is one of the major reasons for ensuring broad consultation with industry in the development of government policy.

The logical rationale is the proportionality principle: the need to distribute costs and burdens in a manner that is proportionate to the specific issue, respective of the fact that the free market most efficiently allocates resources to give us the proper proportionality. Again, a one-size-fits-all approach does not work logically or economically. Failure to ignore the fact that this market is working will adversely impact all businesses as well as governments, especially in developing countries. A harbinger of this failure is the inability of large established telecommunications providers to handle the cost of implementing the regulatory and technological requirements of the Communications and Law Enforcement Assistance Act (CALEA) in the US, even with Federal subsidies.

As a general principle, and specifically in the area of security technologies, government should take a limited, supportive and enabling role in the development of commercial standards, which should emerge from the globally recognized voluntary, industry led, market driven standards process. This is no less true of such sensitive security technology areas as Public Key Infrastructures than for electrical power requirements and network connectivity protocols. Moreover, the role of government-as-customer can not replace, and should not dictate, the voluntary standards process. Inherent in the concept of proportionality is the need to assure that the administrative burdens of record keeping and compliance do not result in unintended consequences that impede the use or deployment of security technology.

A primary role for government is to help raise awareness and to educate all stakeholders. Indeed, if governments are concerned about information security they should work among themselves to improve how they help security in the developing world. There is a definite connection between the digital divide subject and the three pillar topics of cybersecurity, cybercrime and economic security.

It is a critical, though usually unnoticed by many, fact that the Internet was not conceived originally with security in mind. Rather, it was designed to facilitate communication between trusted parties over a trusted network. It was not designed to preclude malicious attackers from defacing networks, stealing personal identities, or from compromising sensitive data. In hindsight, the results of this design strategy are apparent: not only can well-meaning users sometimes impair others' use of the Internet, malicious users can also periodically exploit its inherent weaknesses for financial gain, notoriety, or for the sake of political commentary. From the 'I Love You' computer virus to the cases of distributed denial of service attacks on e-commerce sites to the alteration or defacement of government websites, the threats to the security, privacy and reliability of the Internet are world wide and very significant. These threats have caused damage to stored files, computers, and networks for businesses, governments and individuals, as well as resulting in inconvenience and losses of productivity and credibility. If users cannot trust the Internet and computer networks, e-commerce itself is at risk.

The productivity gains and convenience of this medium may be eviscerated by the threats that exploit its very open nature. Most software and hardware companies work extremely hard to create more secure products, to identify threats and vulnerabilities, to fix problems, and to deliver security solutions. Industry and government are also responding to these threats through such collaborative organizations as ISACs. Many popular web portals loosely collaborate on how to deal with distributed denial of service attacks. But even large sophisticated technology companies face damaging threats.

The Global Internet Project (GIP) review referenced earlier describes the range of threats at a high level; denial of service attacks that flood web sites or ISPs with millions of bogus but apparently legitimate electronic messages that block access to networks and servers; computer break—ins by malicious hackers who violate the confidentiality and integrity of data and systems by exploiting security holes or poorly designed or enforced procedures; internal attacks by disgruntled employees, business partners, and consultants; development and proliferation of destructive computer viruses; and physical attacks on networks and equipment. Storage of data in cached web pages on one's computer and data in commercial data storage facilities create their own set of threats as well. Such storage related threats did not really exist in 1992 and are only being discussed, appreciated, and better understood today.

Given the relentless demand for connectivity to business partners, an attacker's possible points of entry into a network multiply exponentially. For example, stock market operators who may use the Internet to publish their market data live and in real time to their customers work with technology firms to make sure that each broker sees the latest stock price at the same time. If a hacker or virus or denial of service attack were to impact the speed or availability of such data, the functioning of the stock market is challenged. Each link in the security chain is thus weakened by human error, the limits of current technology, and the multiple trust relationships that are required to navigate today's Internet. The most significant threats to the Internet today may best be categorized according to how professional information security measures are implemented to protect against the failure of three information security services:

(1) Confidentiality: Preventing undesired disclosure of information;

(2) Integrity: Preventing undesired modification of information; and

(3) Availability: Preventing an inability to access desired information.

Threats may also be categorized proactively or reactively. Reactive categorization of threats evaluates the symptom (e.g., a tool to exploit a vulnerability) while proactive categorization searches for the underlying cause of the exploit's success.

In contrast to threats, vulnerabilities generally are innate to systems and technology. But with the growing impact of regulation and public policy on the shape of the Internet, some are identifying the fragmented collection of rules and laws at the local, state, national and international levels as well as the custom rules governing networks and sub-networks as vulnerabilities in and of themselves. For example, export controls on strong encryption severely limited the range and strength of possible responses to the vulnerabilities for the network and conflicting rules regarding data preservation and data protection can have a similar effect.

Information Control

Early applications of control focused on the physics of the system being controlled, whether it was the thermal dynamics of buildings, the fight mechanics of an airplane, or the tracking properties of a disk drive head. The situation we now face is one in which pervasive computing, sensing, and communications are common and the way that we interact with machines and they interact with each other is changing rapidly. The consequences of this tremendous increase in information are also manifest in control, where are now facing the challenges of controlling large-scale systems and networks that are well beyond the size and complexity of the traditional applications of control. One indication of this shift is the role that embedded systems and software play in modern technology.

Modern computer control systems are capable of enormous amounts of decision making and control logic. Increasingly, these software systems are interacting with physical processes and introducing feedback algorithms to improve performance and robustness. Already, the amount of logic-based code is overshadowing the traditional control algorithms in many applications. Much of this logic is interwoven with the closed loop performance of the system, but systematic methods for analysis, verification, and design have yet to be developed. Another area where control of information-based systems will be increasingly important is in resource allocation systems. In this context, control can be described as the science and engineering of optimal dynamic resource allocation under uncertainty. Uncertainty is critical: there is some possible variation in the system's behavior, so that decisions have to be made taking different possibilities into account. Sources of uncertainty include incomplete or corrupted information available to the decision maker, uncertainty in the mathematical model used to model the system, and unpredictability of commands due to noise and disturbance signals that affect the system. While often considered an operations research problem, the role of dynamics and instabilities points to a clear need for control theory as well.

One of the consequences of this shift toward information-based systems is that are moving from an era where physics was the bottleneck to progress to one in which complexity is the bottleneck. There are already many examples of this new class of systems that are being deployed. Congestion control in routers for the Internet, power control in wireless communications systems, and real-time use of information in service and supply chains are a few examples. In all of these systems, it is the interaction of information flow with the underlying physics that is responsible for the overall performance. Another example is the air trafic control network, where the density of fights, demand for efficiency, and intolerance for failure have created a situation that couples vast amounts of information—everything from the location of the planes to the individual customer itineraries—that must be managed to maintain high performance, robust, and reliable operation at all times. There is an important role for control in many of these applications. As in traditional application areas, control serves as a mechanism for getting both information and, more importantly, action out of data. Furthermore, the theory of control provides insights and tools for analyzing and designing interconnected systems with desirable stability and robustness properties. One fundamental change in the use of control is the role of communications and networking. This will radically change the use of feedback in modern systems, through increased access to large amounts of information as well as the new environment in which control systems will have to operate.

Control computations must increasingly be done in a distributed, partially asynchronous environment where tight control over the timing of data and computation is not available, due for example to the existence of packet-based communications networks between sensing, actuation, and computational nodes. Many traditional approaches may no longer work in this context and we anticipate the need to develop new paradigms for designing robust, high performance, feedback systems in this information rich environment. The role of uncertainty in information rich systems is also critical (and largely unexplored) and concepts from control will play an important role in managing this uncertainty in the analysis, design, and operation of large-scale, interconnected systems. Uncertainty must be represented in order to build tractable models for answering questions that take into account the whole range of possible variations in the details of components and their interconnections.

Control ideas will be increasingly important as a tool for managing both the complexity and uncertainty in these systems, and must be made available to the designers of such systems, through education and design software. One aspect of this that is likely to be particularly important is the exploration of fundamental limits of performance, robustness, and stability, since tradeoffs between these will be the primary design challenge in this space. Examples of the need for increased development in this area can be seen in the applications discussed in the next chapter. Vehicle, mission, and airspace management systems for transportation; source, power, and router control for networks; and genetic, cellular, and integrative feedback networks in biological systems are just a few examples.

The simplest of these problems lies at the boundaries of current tools and understanding, and future progress will require a much deeper understanding of the integration between control, communications, computing, and networks as well as modeling, analysis, and control of complex decision systems.

Opportunities and Challenges

Control has developed into a major field in which generations of engineers are able to solve problems of practical importance and enormous impact. Over the past few years, the opportunities for control have expanded enormously, but there are many challenges that must be addressed to realize the potential for impact. The characterize some of the overarching themes that describe these opportunities and challenges, and recommend an approach for moving forward.

The future of control will be driven by a new environment that differs substantially from that of the past 40 years. Some of the features of this new environment are already apparent and provide insight into the new research directions that must be pursued. Ubiquitous Computation, Communication and Sensing. The dominant change in the engineering environment is the presence of ever more powerful computation and cheaper communication. The new software and storage products that these developments have spawned have further changed the engineering landscape in many areas. It will require decades to take full advantage of these developments. Some innovation will involve standalone improvements to individual systems and some will involve extreme interconnectedness of the type seen in the telephone system, the power grid, the Internet, and their descendants. Both types may, and probably will, depend on the use of control. The new ideas required to be successful in the two cases are, however, likely to be qualitatively different because we do not yet have a great deal of experience in building and operating safe, reliable, highly interconnected systems.

New application domains: In addition to the revolutionary changes in information technology, future control systems will involve interactions between physical, chemical, biological, and information sciences, integrated with algorithms and feedback. This will open up new application domains for control, such as biological engineering and quantum systems. While there are already researchers within the control community that are attacking problems in these areas, it will be necessary to educate new generations of researchers in both control and other disciplines in order to make advances in these applications. The possibilities for control are potentially very fundamental in nature, as illustrated in the following vignette.

Reliable systems with unreliable parts: Most reasonably complex man-made systems are not rendered inoperable by the failure of any particular component and biological systems often demonstrate remarkable robustness in this regard. Simple redundancy, or the spare parts approach to such problems, is of limited effectiveness because it is uneconomical. Designs that allow the system to reconfigure itself when a component fails, even if this degrades the performance roughly in proportion to the magnitude of the failure, are usually preferred. Although computer memory chips and disk drive controllers often take advantage of strategies of this type, it is still true that the design of self healing systems is not well studied or analyzed. This issue takes on considerable significance when dealing with interconnected systems of the complexity of the Internet. In this case there are billions of components and yet the system is so essential that little downtime can be tolerated.

Complexity: Air traffic control systems, power grid control systems and other large-scale, interconnected systems are typical of a class of problems whose complexity is fixed not by the designer but rather by economic considerations and the natural scale of the problem. An acceptable solution in this context must be capable of dealing with the given complexity. In deciding if a system can be built or not, it is important to correctly gauge the feasibility because there is no value in a product that "almost "works. Every discipline has methods for dealing with some types of complexity. In the physical sciences, for example, the tools developed for studying statistical mechanics have lead to a very substantial body of literature, effective for solving some problems. However, in discussing complexity it is one thing to find a point of view from which aspects of the behavior is compressible but it is another to have a "theory of complex systems ".

The latter is something of an oxymoron, in that it suggests that the system is not really complex. On the other hand, it does make sense to seek to understand and organize the methodologies which have proven to be useful in the design of highly interconnected systems and to study naturally occurring systems with this in mind. Engineers looking at the immune system may very well be able to suggest new methods to defeat Internet viruses and ideas from neuroscience may inspire new developments in building reliable systems using unreliable components.

This new environment for control presents many challenges, but also many opportunities for impact across a broad variety of application areas. The future directions in control, dynamics, and systems must continue to address fundamental issues, guided by new applications. One of the biggest challenges facing the field is the integration of computation, communications, and control. As computing, communications, and sensing become more ubiquitous, the use of control will become increasingly ubiquitous as well. However, many of the standard paradigms that allow the separation of these different disciplines will no longer be valid. For example, the ability to separate the computational architecture from the functions that are being computed is already beginning to unravel as we look at distributed systems with redundant, intermittent, and sometimes unreliable computational elements. Beyond simply looking at hybrid systems, a theory must be developed that integrates computer science and control.

Similarly, the simplification that two nodes that are connected can communicate with sufficient reliability and bandwidth such that the properties of the communications channel can be ignored no longer holds in the highly networked environment of the future. Control must become more integrated with the protocols of communications so that high response feedback loops are able to use the same channels as high throughput, lower bandwidth information, without interfering with each other. Another element of the future of control is to begin to understand analysis and synthesis of control using higher levels of decision making. Traditionally control has dealt with the problem of keeping a few variables constant (regulation) or making variables follow specified time functions (tracking). In robotics, control was faced with more complicated problems such as obstacle avoidance and path planning (task-based control). Future systems will require that control be applied to problems that cannot necessarily be expressed in terms of continuous variables, but rather have symbolic, linguistic, or protocol-based descriptions. This is required as we move to more sophisticated autonomous and semi-autonomous systems that require high-level decision making capabilities.

At the same time as control moves to higher levels of decision making, it will also move to new domains that are only beginning to emerge at the present time. This includes biological, quantum and environmental systems; software systems; enterprise level systems; and economic and financial systems. In all of these new problem domains, it will be necessary to develop a rigorous theory of control. This has been a historical strength of the field and has allowed it to be successful in an enormous number of systems. Finally, we envision an increased awareness of control principles in science and engineering, including much more exposure to feedback systems in math and science education.

A typical congested gateway looks like a fire hose connected to a soda straw through a small funnel (the output queue). If, on average, packets arrive faster than they can leave, the funnel will fill up and eventually over flow. RED [Random Early Detection] is [a]simple regulator that monitors the level in the funnel and uses it to match the input rate to the output (by dropping excess traffic). As long as its control law is monotone non-decreasing and covers the full range of 0 to 100% drop rate, RED works for any link, any bandwidth, any type of traffic. North American Network Operators 'Group meeting, 1998. The rapid growth of communications networks provides several major opportunities and challenges for control. Although there is overlap, we can divide these roughly into two main areas: control of networks and control over networks.

Control of Networks

Control of networks is a large area, spanning many topics, a few of which are briefly described here. The basic problems in control of networks include controlling congestion across network links, routing the flow of packets through the network, caching and updating data at multiple locations, and managing power levels for wireless networks. Several features of these control problems make them very challenging. The dominant feature is the extremely large scale of the system; the Internet is probably the largest feedback control system man has ever built. Another is the decentralized nature of the control problem: local decisions must be made quickly, and based only on local information. Stability is complicated by the presence of varying time lags, as information about the network state can only be observed or relayed to controllers after a time delay, and the effect of a local control action can be felt throughout the network after substantial delay. Uncertainty and variation in the network, through network topology, transmission channel characteristics, traffic demand, available resources, etc. , may change constantly and unpredictably.

Another complicating issue is the diverse traffic characteristics, in terms of arrival statistics at both the packet and flow time scales, and different requirements for quality of service, in terms of delay, bandwidth, and loss probability, that the network must support. Resources that must be managed in this environment include computing, storage and transmission capacities at end hosts and routers. Performance of such systems is judged in many ways: throughput, delay, loss rates, fairness, reliability, as well as the speed and quality with which the network adapts to changing traffic patterns, changing resource availability, and changing network congestion. To illustrate these characteristics, we briefly describe the control mechanisms that can be invoked in serving a file request from a client: network caching, congestion control, routing and power control.

When the document is requested, it is returned by the nearest server. Here, proximity may be measured by geographical distance, hop count, network congestion, server load or a combination. The goal is to reduce delay, relieve server load, balance network traffic, and improve service reliability. If changes are made to the source document, those changes (at a minimum) must be transmitted to the servers, which consume network bandwidth. The control problem is to devise a decentralized scheme for how often to update, where to cache copies of documents, and to which server a client request is directed, based on estimation and prediction of access patterns, network congestion, and server load. Clearly, current decisions affect the future state, such as future traffic on links, future buffer levels, delay and congestion, and server load. Thus a web of caches is a decentralized feedback system that is spatially distributed and interconnected, where control decisions are made asynchronously based on local and delayed information. When a large file is requested, the server that is selected to return the file breaks it into a stream of packets and transports them to the client in a rate-adaptive manner. This process is governed by the Transport Control Protocol (TCP). The client acknowledges successful reception of each packet and the stream of acknowledgment carries congestion information to the server.

Congestion control is a distributed algorithm to share network resources among competing servers. It consists of two components: a source algorithm that dynamically adjusts the server rate in response to congestion in its path, and a router algorithm that updates a congestion measure and sends it back to sources that go through that router. Examples of congestion measures are loss probability and queuing delay. They are implicitly updated at the routers and implicitly fed back to sources through delayed end-to-end observations of packet loss or delay. The equilibrium and dynamics of the network depends on the pair of source and router algorithms. A good way to understand the system behavior is to regard the source rates as primal variables and router congestion measures as dual variables, and the process of congestion control as an asynchronous distributed primal-dual algorithm carried out by sources and routers over the Internet in real time to maximize aggregate source utility subject to resource capacity constraints. Different protocols all solve the same prototypical problem, but they use different utility functions and implement different iterative rules to optimize them. While TCP controls the rate of a packet flow, the path through the network is controlled by the Internet Protocol (IP). In its simplest form, each router must decide which output link a given packet will be sent to on its way to its final destination. Uncertainties include varying link congestion, delays, and rates, and even varying network topology (e. g. , a link goes down, or new nodes or links become available), as well as future traffic levels. A routing algorithm is an asynchronous distributed algorithm executed at routers that adapts to node and link failures, balances network traffic and reduces congestion. It can be decomposed into several time scales, with very fast decisions made in hardware using lookup tables, which in turn are updated on a slower time scale. At the other extreme in time scale from the routing problem, we have optimal network planning, in which new links and nodes are proposed to meet predicted future traffic demand. The routing problem is further exacerbated in wireless networks.

Nodes with wireless modems may be mobile, and the address of a node may neither indicate where it is located nor how to reach it. Thus the network needs to either search for a node on demand, or it must keep track of the changing locations of nodes. Further, since link capacities in wireless networks may be scarce, routing may have to be determined in conjunction with some form of load balancing. This gives rise to the need for distributed asynchronous algorithms which are adaptive to node locations, link failures, mobility, and changes in traffic flow requirements. Finally, if the client requesting the file accesses it through an ad hoc wireless network, then there also arises the problem of power control: at what transmission power level should each packet broadcast be made? Power control is required because ad hoc networks do not come with ready made links; the topology of the network is formed by individual nodes choosing the power levels of their broadcasts. This poses a conceptual problem in the current protocol hierarchy of the Internet since it simultaneously affects the physical layer due to its effect on signal quality, the network layer since power levels determine which links are available for traffic to be routed, and the transport layer since power levels of broadcasts affect congestion.

Power control is also a good challenge for multi-objective control since there are many cost criteria involved, such as increasing the traffic carrying capacity of the network, reducing the battery power used in relaying traffic, and reducing the contention for the common shared medium by the nodes in geographical vicinity. Control of networks extends beyond data and communication networks. Optimal routing and flow control of commercial aircraft (with emphasis on guaranteeing safe inter-vehicle distances) will help maximize utilization of airports. The (network and software) infrastructure for supply chain systems is being built right now, and simple automated supply chain management systems are beginning to be deployed. In the near future, sophisticated optimization and control methods can be used to direct the flow of goods and money between suppliers, assemblers and processors, and customers.

While the advances in information technology to date have led to a global Internet that allows users to exchange information, it is clear that the next phase will involve much more interaction with the physical environment. Networks of sensory or actuator nodes with computational capabilities, connected wirelessly or by wires, can form an orchestra which controls physical environment. Examples include automobiles, smart homes, large manufacturing systems, intelligent highways and networked city services, and enterprise-wide supply and logistics chains. Thus, this next phase of the information technology revolution is the convergence of communication, computing and control. The following vignette describes a major architectural challenge in achieving this convergence. As existing networks continue to build out, and network technology becomes cheaper and more reliable than fixed point-to-point connections, even in small lo-calized systems, more and more control systems will operate over networks. We can foresee sensor, actuator, diagnostic, and command and coordination signals all traveling over data networks. The estimation and control functions can be distributed across multiple processors, also linked by data networks.

Current control systems are almost universally based on synchronous, clocked systems, so they require communications networks that guarantee delivery of sensor, actuator, and other signals with a known, fixed delay. While current control systems are robust to variations that are included in the design process (such as a variation in some aerodynamic coefficient, motor constant, or moment of inertia), they are not at all tolerant of (unmodeled) communication delays, or dropped or lost sensor or actuator packets. Current control system technology is based on a simple communication architecture: all signals travel over synchronous dedicated links, with known (or worst-case bounded) delays, and no packet loss.

Clearly, several fundamental control concepts will not make the transition to an asynchronous, packet-based environment. The most obvious casualty will be the transfer function, and all the other concepts associated with linear time invariant (LTI) systems (impulse and step response, frequency response, spectrum, bandwidth, etc.) This is not a small loss, as this has been a foundation of control engineering since about 1930. With the loss goes a lot of intuition and understanding. For example, Bode plots were introduced in the 1930s to understand and design feedback amplifiers, were updated to handle discrete-time control systems in the 1960s. Even the optimal control methods in the 1960s, which appeared at first to be quite removed from frequency domain concepts, were shown to be nicely interpreted via transfer functions.

So what methods will make the transition? Many of the methods related to optimai control and optimal dynamic resource allocation will likely transpose gracefully to an asynchronous, packet-based environment. Another idea that will gracefully extend to asynchronous packet-based control is model predictive control. The basic idea is to carry out far more computation at run time, by solving optimization problems in the real-time feedback control law. Model predictive control has played a major role in process control, and also in supply-chain management, but not (yet) in other areas, mainly owing to the very large computational burden it places on the controller implementation. The idea is very simple: at each time step we formulate the optimal control problem, up to some time horizon in the future, and solve for the whole optimal trajectory. We then use the current optimal input as the actuator signal. The sensor signals can be used to update the model, and carry the same process out again. A major extension required to apply model predictive control in networked environments would be the distributed solution of the underlying optimization problem.

While we have concentrated in this section on the role of control in communications and networking, there are many problems in the broader field of information science and technology for which control ideas will be important. We highlight a few here; more information can also be found in a recent National Research Council report on embedded systems. Vigilant, high confidence software systems Modern information systems are required to operate in environments where the users place high confidence on the availability and correctness of the software programs. This is increasingly difficult due to the networked and often adversarial environment in which these programs operate. One approach that is being explored by the computer science community is to provide confidence through vigilance. The key idea in vigilant software is to use fast and accurate sensing to monitor the execution of a system or algorithm, compare the performance of the algorithm to an embedded model of the computation, and then modify the operation of the algorithm (through adjustable parameters) to maintain the desired performance. This 'sense-compute-act' loop is the basic paradigm of feedback control and provides a mechanism for online management of uncertainty. Its power lies in the fact that rather than considering every possible situation at design time, the system reacts to specific situations as they occur. An essential element of the strategy is the use of either an embedded model, through which an appropriate control action can be determined. or a predefined control strategy that is analyzed offine to ensure stability, performance, and robustness.

While unconventional from a traditional computer science perspective, this approach gives robustness to failure of individual sorters, as well as self-reconfiguring operation. Robustness comes because if an individual module unsorts its data, this data will not be selected from the input streams by the other modules. Further, if the modules have different loads (perhaps due to other processing being done on a given processor), the module with the most time available will automatically take on the load in performing the distributed sorting. Other properties such as disturbance rejection, performance, and stability could also be studied by using tools from control.

Verification and validation of protocols and software: The development of complex software systems is increasing at a rapid rate and our ability to design such systems so that they give provably correct performance is increasingly strained. Current methods for verification and validation of software systems require large amounts of testing and many errors are not discovered until late stages of development or even product release. Formal methods for verification of software are used for systems of moderate complexity, but do not scale well to large software systems. Control theory has developed a variety of techniques for giving provably correct behavior by using upper and lower bounds to effectively break computational complexity bounds. Recent results in convex optimization of semialgebraic problems (those that can be expressed by polynomial equalities and inequalities) are providing new insights into verification of a diverse set of continuous and combinatorial optimization problems. In particular, these new techniques allow a systematic search for "simple proofs "of mixed continuous and discrete problems and offer ideas for combining formal methods in computer science with stability and robustness results in control.

Real-time supply chain management As increasing numbers of enterprise systems are connected to each other across networks, there is an enhanced ability to perform enterprise level, dynamic recon figuration of high availability assets for achieving efficient, reliable, predictable operations. As an example of the type of application that one can imagine, consider the operation of a network of HVAC systems for a regional collection of buildings, under the control of a single operating company. In order to minimize overall energy costs for its operation, the company makes a long-term arrangement with an energy broker to supply a specified amount of electrical power that will be used to heat and cool the buildings. In order to get the best price for the energy it purchases, the company agrees to purchase a fixed amount of energy across its regional collection of buildings and to pay a premium for energy usage above this amount. This gives the energy broker a fixed income as well as a fixed (maximum) demand, for which it is willing to sell electricity at a lower price (due to less uncertainty in future revenue as well as system loading).

Due to the uncertainty in the usage of the building, the weather in different areas across the region, and the reliability of the HVAC subsystems in the buildings, a key element in implementing such an arrangement is a distributed, real-time command and control system capable of performing distributed optimization of interconnected assets. The power broker and the company must be able to communicate information about asset condition and mission between the control systems for their electrical generation and HVAC systems and the subsystems must react to sensed changes in the environment (occupancy, weather, equipment status) to optimize the fleet level performance of the network. Realization of enterprise-wide optimization of this sort will require substantial progress in a number of technical areas: distributed, embedded modeling tools that allow low resolution modeling of the external system combined with high resolution modeling of the local system, resident at each node in the enterprise; distributed optimization algorithms that make use of the embedded modeling architecture to produce near optimal operations; fault tolerant, networked control systems that allow control loops to operate across unreliable network connections; and low cost, fault tolerant, recon figurable hardware and software architectures. A very closely related problem is that of C4ISR (command, control, communication, computers, intelligence, surveillance, and reconnaissance) in military systems. Here also, networked systems are revolutionizing the capabilities for continuous planning and asset allocation, but new research is needed in providing robust solutions that give the required performance in the presence of uncertainty and adversaries. The underlying issues and techniques are almost identical to enterprise level resource allocation, but the environment in which they must perform is much more challenging for military applications. Control concepts will be essential tools for providing robust performance in such dynamic, uncertain, and adversarial environments.

5

ICT Growth in India

The 21st century witnesses realistic opportunities for developing countries and transition economies to play a qualitatively new role in the world economic landscape. Some developing countries have become aware of the new advantages ICT may bring, given its top priority. India's unique experience in Information Technology (IT) is definitely worth studying. With its population mostly illiterate, initial investment opportunities limited and its investment climate volatile, this vast and predominantly poor developing country, within a short time, succeeded in building a powerful IT industry and its software export sector, in particular. This has been made possible due to the Indian Government's policies that strongly support IT development, activities of Indian businessmen, and certain advantages this country enjoys.

According to International Data Corporation (IDC) and Digital Planet 2000 , the global ICT market in 1999 has surpassed the U.S.$ 2 trillion mark and keeps growing at an average of 9% p.a. It is projected to reach U.S.$ 3 trillion by 2003-2004. Many countries are making huge ICT investments, in particular, in building and supporting infrastructure, developing partnerships and training personnel to promote further ICT growth. North America remains the world's largest regional ICT market whose market share was U.S.$ 796 billion in 1999. ICT per capita spending can now determine the socio-economic development of nations.

In the early years of the computer industry, manufacturers supplied all the required software 'free' with their machines. IBM realized in the late 1960s that software could become a golden stream of new revenues, and it started to charge separately for hardware and software. By doing so, it gave birth to the independent software industry, giving other companies a chance to supply programs for IBM computers more efficiently than IBM itself. After a modest start of the 60s, growth in the world software market became almost exponential from the late 70s onwards: indeed, in 1978 the global software market was estimated at $2.5 billion, while in 1985 it already reached $25 billion.

The IT development shows a sustained tendency to increase the percentage of software and services as compared to that of hardware in the total cost of computer products. Thus, while in 1960 about 80% of the cost was hardware and only 20% - software and services, currently this ratio is changing in favor of software: various sources estimate the cost of software and services today at 60 to 80% of the total cost of IT products. The IT boom and ever increasing demand for IT services have caused some problems in industrialized economies. The most important of them are:

— Rising development costs,

— Shortage of skilled personnel.

Telecommunications and the Internet, alongside the standardization of software production, programming languages and hardware brought about sufficient stability in software and services production technologies and experience. This stability made it possible to outsource projects, i.e. to involve other companies in the development of projects or of their separate stages. On the one hand, the outsourcing of projects promotes greater division of labor among separate companies and, thus, provides a source for productivity growth. On the other hand, the shortage of IT specialists resulting from a strong demand for information technology and IT services, opens up opportunities to make the entire production process internationalized and globalized through outsourcing.

Remote access to information, and prospects for globalization of the qualified labor market make it possible to project a drastic change in the economic growth rates of the world's least developed countries. Surging development of computer and information technologies and their cheaper costs are creating prerequisites for integrating developing countries into the global post-industrialized economic landscape. Software and services production is an absolutely special industry that requires large labor costs and intellectual investments in an absolutely special "virtual product". It is not as capital intensive as other IT branches. Thus, unlike hardware production, software development calls for much smaller investments in equipping job places and in direct organization of the technological process. This is the reason why the development of this branch of the IT industry creates more favorable opportunities for integrating developing countries and transition economies in the global ICT production complex.

The last decades of the second millennium saw high growth rates of the software and services industry in such countries as India, China, Brazil, Mexico, Singapore, Hong Kong, Taiwan, South Korea, and the Philippines. India occupies a special place among these countries. On the one hand, this was caused by the fact that among the Third World countries India has the largest software industry with the longest history. On the other hand, India has been pursuing a government policy in software and services production since 1 970, which is much earlier than in any other developing country.

India provides a vivid example of a developing country integrating in the global information community. Within a comparatively short time, this country has been able to build a powerful IT industry, has literally become the Third World's computer colossus and is targeting for a leading position in the global IT market. India's relatively long history of IT development can provide useful lessons for other countries looking for guidelines in developing their IT industries and especially software industries.

IT is now on the lips of every educated Indian, mainly due to the global success of India's export-led software industry. The industry's huge potential in generating wealth, hard currency inflow and new job opportunities has already caught the imagination of India's businessmen, individuals, economists, bureaucracy and politicians. With software production as its prime-mover, India's IT industry is a priority of the national economy and justly draws everybody's attention as an instrument and a pattern to transform the entire Indian economy.

Recent historical evidence provides little support for the view that market forces alone can be left to determine the size, composition and characteristics of a country's industrial sector. It can be argued that governments in at least the majority of developing countries ought to retain some responsibilities for the process of industrialization. Yet, this does not apply to developing countries only: the U.S. IT industry is known to have been government-funded in the 40s, 50s and 60s, when a strong inflow of capital was critical for the industry development. Now, with its feet firm on the ground and U.S. software products highly competitive in the global market, the U.S.

IT industry development is determined by market forces. And the U.S. Government has always been actively assisting the industry development: suffice it to say that it was the Government that funded the Internet development and is currently involved in funding the Internet 2 project; another example is ARPA (Advanced Research Projects Agency) investments in IT R&D, which in the 90s amounted to hundreds of millions of US dollars. In all countries governments are the largest consumer of IT products and services. Thus, the U.S. government sector consumes 23% of IT national consumption, and in India this figure is about 28%. Thus, government demand for IT products and services in many respects affects the areas of IT industry development. By formulating and pursuing certain economic, legal and taxation policies, by setting priorities, the governments cannot but intervene in or influence the development of economic industries in their countries.

The government has three roles to play in economic development – that of a regulator, of a promoter and of a producer. *The East Asia Miracle*—a study published by the

World Bank in 1993, stressed the need to formulate clear-cut government policies to intensify the IT industry development. India exemplifies a country where the government has been strongly supporting software and services development.

Software Development

The Indian Government's active interventions in software industry development aimed to minimize these constraints and their negative implications for the industry development. The current surge of India's software industry, given the country's narrow domestic market and a low level of economic development, has become possible due to the government policies of incentives for science-intensive technology exports, and in particular, for software and services exports. As a result the IT industry has become markedly export-oriented.

In the mid-60s, the Indian government's industrial policies showed some signs of liberalization, departure from rigid planning and an emphasis on exports, while the government policy's principal elements remained unchanged. At that time hardware was predominantly imported. In the 1970s, the government tried to intensify domestic hardware production by tough regulatory measures and by reducing hardware imports. By encouraging software production the Government primarily aimed to create conditions for exporting producers to be supplied with imported hardware. In the mid of 1970, the Department of Electronics was established, whose responsibilities were to promote the software industry and to formulate policies for its development. In the early 70s, the DoE approved some export developing programs. Thus, in 1972 it adopted the "Software Export Scheme" that allowed hardware imports in order to produce software under certain export obligations.

The year 1974 can be regarded as the year of birth for Indian software exports: it was the first time in history when the Indian company - Tata Consultancy Services (TCS) - took a decision to export software in order to import hardware. That period was described as a "law-making" time and, indeed, some specific measures were taken to give momentum to the development of the industry:

— The DoE invested significant funds in scientific research projects carried out by public enterprises involved in software development.

— Government support was provided to Indian companies – software developers (who actually adjusted imported software products).

— The government supported the system of higher computer education to enable it to meet the modern standards of the industry development.

In 1976, the industrial policy was in part liberalized. Customs duties on imported hardware were reduced from 100% to 40%. Banks were recommended to extend loan terms for software producers. Software exporters were promised faster customs clearance, besides they were allowed to be located in EPZs (Export Processing Zone) whose taxation was preferential and export-import procedures organized. Software exporters began to get cash compensatory support - 8% of their total exports. On the other hand, the Indian Government pursued the policy of encouraging domestic producers of hardware by limiting activities and rights of foreign importers. The Government exerted pressure on foreign companies by making them continuously improve their technological process, pay for the entire import with equivalent exports, and reduce their share in Indian companies, etc. These measures resulted in IBM departure from India in 1978 and consequently in the inflow of 2,000 ex-IBM skilled specialists to the Indian labor market. This had a positive impact on the industry development, since many of them had good managerial skills and set up their own companies.

Between 1980 and 1984, some measures were taken to toughen control over hardware imports. To boost domestic production, customs duties for imported hardware were raised to 135%, and export enterprises were recommended to import hardware under a new pattern – by leasing. In 1981, the Ministry of Trade established the status of an export-oriented unit - EOU (Export-Oriented Units). By their rights and benefits EOUs were placed on the same footing as EPZs, but unlike them EOUs lacked in developed infrastructure. Despite toughened policies to lower the abuse of the then export-import legislation, the DoE further promoted conditions for software and services export growth. For example, it was at that time that the Engineering Export Promotion Council began to assist software and services exporters in marketing. Later the Trade Development Authority was entrusted with these functions.

By 1984, it became clear that the government policies failed to meet the requirements of the developing industry and there was an urgent need to work out a new concept. It took quite a long time to develop New

Computer Policy. Its draft was approved in November 1984 – a few days after Rajiv Gandhi was elected Prime Minister. An ardent supporter of computerization and high technologies, the new Prime Minister came to power at a time when IBM-compatible PCs emerged in the Indian market. While the main points of the New Program addressed computer production in India, it also included measures to liberalize the software and services industry. In particular, it aimed:

— To simplify procedures related to hardware imports;

— To reduce the price of imported hardware by lowering the basic customs duty on imported hardware from 135% to 60%, and on some peripherals from 80% to 5%;

— To lower duties on imported software from 100% to 60% and to permit duty-free imports of source code software on paper;

— To recognize software production as an industry and to delicense software development;

— To simplify procedures related to hard currency accounts and transactions;

— To allow the use of international telecom links to export software and services;

— To place software under the Copyright Act.

— Government software policy in the making: Rajiv Gandhi and his coterie

The role of certain government officials interested in formulating the present-day policy targeting for the country's leading position in information technology deserves special attention.

It was then – in the mid-80s – that the basis for India's industrial policy in software production was laid, which prompted its further boom. A key role in formulating the main areas of this policy was played by Dr. H. Seshagiri, the DoE Additional Secretary, who between 1984-1986 was the moving spirit and architect behind the government liberalization policy in the software industry. Sincere, determined and actively committed to liberalization, Dr. Seshagiri saw India's future as that of a strong competitive software power and tried to implement his beliefs. In his words, by developing software exports India gets access to a vast economic and technological potential, which will obviously benefit the country. Rajiv Gandhi, as Prime Minister, took a personal interest in the liberalization of industrial software policy.

In the mid-1980s, some ministers and advisers supported the development of the software industry. Among them was Vishvanat Pratap Singh, who was Finance Minister during the early part of Rajiv Gandhi's tenure. That support had an important impact, since Dr. Seshagiri's activities to liberalize India's industrial policies were opposed by some government officials. Some of Dr. Seshagiri's initiatives failed to be implemented at that time, however they laid the basis for further reforms made in India in the late 80s and the early 90s. It was this man's efforts that provided a foundation for the further development of the DoE and for its transformation into a promoter of the software industry, into a technocratic rather than bureaucratic authority.

In 1986, India made the development of the software industry one of the economic priority areas. The Indian Government developed the program: Policy on Computer

Software Export, Software Development and Training. Under this program, hardware imports were made easier through some procedural changes, and regulations on domestic-oriented use of imported hardware were dropped. The import of software was also delicensed (changed from quota to tariff protection) so that anyone could import it if they paid the 60 per cent import duty. However, hardware imports became more risky because the attached export obligations were strengthened.

Software exporters' cash compensatory support was raised to 10% of their total exports. In 1986, the Software Development Agency (SDA) was set up within the DoE. The new structure was designed to formulate, implement and coordinate government software policies and also to assist the country's software industry development. In 1986, the DoE came up with its favorite brainchild – its first Software Technology Parks. Their aim was to promote offshore programming and get faster and easier access to international telecommunications. Under certain terms and export-import obligations, the STP status can be given both to an individual company and to an entire industrial zone locating multitudes of companies. STP rights and benefits in international economic activities and in tax concessions were equal to those of EPZs and acquired the status of EPZs under the DoE control.

Import liberalization was needed to make use of the world's advanced high-tech achievements. This, in turn, helped India:

— overcome technological barriers in offshore software development;

— fill the gap between world technologies and pricing and India's ones;

— increase productivity and improve software production quality;

— increase software exports considerably.

According to some Indian industrial officials and international observers, that period is described as departure from a clear-cut liberalization in India's entire government industrial policy, which also affected government policies toward the software industry. The then government measures can be described as "one step forward two steps back". However, by the end of that period software and services exports in India were regulated by the following provisions:

— "10 crore rule". Any large company exporting more than Rs. 100 million of software could pay off its export obligations in whatever manner it chose, while smaller companies were restricted to exports that made use of the imported computer which had attracted the export obligations in the first place.

— New hardware import conditions, differentiated export obligations and customs tariffs. Thus, for EPZs, EOUs and STPs hardware imports had zero customs duties, while for the remaining enterprises:

— Loaned computer systems could be imported:

— for 6 months, with an export obligation of 25% depending on the cost of the imported hardware, and customs duties were 18%; for 1 year, with 50% and 20% respectively.

— The bigger obligations the companies assumed, the lower customs duties for imported hardware they paid:

— If export obligations were high (350% of the imported hardware value) customs duties were 35%;

— If export obligations were low (250% of the imported hardware value) customs duties were 65 %.

— Software import duties were established at 107%.

From 1987, software companies had to register with the DoE to receive certain export promotion assistance. The export turnover threshold for those eligible to register was reduced from Rs. 5 million in 1987 to Rs.0.2million in 1989. An insurance scheme was introduced in 1987 to cover the clients of Indian software companies against malpractice, besides, export shipment credit and credit guarantees were made available. During the same period venture capital funding for software companies was first introduced.

In 1986, India launched a telecommunications satellite to ensure fast communications between their software R&D companies and their overseas clients. In 1987, a Bangalore branch of the U.S. company Texas Instruments installed the first land-based satellite communication station in India to organize export-import transactions related to software developmen\. In 1988, the government set up the Electronics and Computer Export Promotion Council to support electronics and software exporters mainly in the area of marketing. Late in 1990, the software industry was wholly exempted from tax on export profits received from software and services exports.

In 1990, the concept of software technology parks took more specific shape of Software Technology Parks of

India (STPI) Scheme, under which the STP status of an export processing zone under DoE was reaffirmed. Early in 1991, software imports became more problematic. This was caused by the rupee devaluation and more stringent import policies.

In the middle of 1991, with new Prime Minister Narasimha Rao and new Finance Minister Manmohan Singh in power, India started a new phase of its development – a liberalization boost in the entire industrial policy. Manmohan Singh had received Western education, for some time he had worked for the World Bank, had liberal views which he actively implemented when he was Finance Minister. In that period, private capital was allowed access to most industries. Many foreign trade barriers were lowered. Lists of imported goods subject to licensing were shortened. Foreign investment policies were liberalized especially with respect to institutionalized investors and non-resident Indians. Acceptable ratio of exports to domestic sales was established for exporters. Foreign capital share was increased to 51%, and for exporters - to 100%.

In 1991, N.Vittal was appointed the DoE Secretary. In many respects due to his activities in software policy-making some software-related measures were adopted. They encouraged the industry's further development. Among the most important measures were the following:

Reduction in telecommunications charges for satellite links;

— Duty-free, obligation-free import of telecommunications equipment into EPZs, STPs, etc.;

— Confirmation of exemption from profit tax on software and services exports;

— Zero excise rates from software sold;

— Export obligations can be met from earnings of the staff sent to work overseas at the client's site.

From the mid-80s, the World Bank actively promoted India's software development by funding and supporting government reforms and changes in finances, education and marketing. Namely, in 1990-1991, technical training support projects were approved. Under the projects, the Indian Department of Education was to receive U.S.$ 567 million during 8 years. In 1992, the World Bank developed the IT strategy it recommended to India, where it defined the guidelines for government-encouraged growth and improvement of IT production.Late in 1992, the Department of Electronics was reorganized to increase its role of a promotional body for the software industry. The process included:

— Change and update of DoE training policies;

— Change and update of DoE R&D policies;

— Changes and amendments in the Copyright Act to toughen punishment for illegal software production and software piracy.

Import policies were changed: customs duties for software imports were reduced from 112% in 1991:

— to 110% in 1992,

— to 85% in 1993,

— to 20% for applications and to 65% for systems software in 1994,

— to 10% for all software in 1995.

In 1992, India's IT industry marked a remarkable event: for the first time an Indian software producing company received ISO 9001 certification. The pioneer company that opened the way for many other Indian companies was International Informatics Solutions. From 1993, the government in every way encouraged Indian software companies to obtain international certifications like ISO 9000,and others. In April 1993, India permitted reproduction of imported software by agreement with foreign partners. If the author's share of a foreign company was less than 30%, there was no need for a preliminary DoE permission to organize production. In September 1995, India adopted a regulation which made individuals, firms and companies working abroad under software and services contracts return to India at least 30% of the contract amount. In the same period, new high export obligations were introduced – 400% for a 5-year period, which made it possible to import hardware and pay 15% customs duty.

In 1998, Prime Minister Atal Bihari Vajpayee said in his first televised address to the Indian people that the development of the IT industry was one of the five national priorities and declared that India was targeting for the status of a global IT superpower. In April 1998 at an annual . II (the Confederation of Indian Industry) session, the Prime Minister stressed that IT production was the only sphere where India would be able to rate among the superpowers due to the country's high competitiveness. In the same year, the IT Task Force"8 was set up by the Government.

The IT Task Force launched India's software development program for the next decade (up to the year 2008) - Information Technology Action Plan This plan is being implemented now. The Indian IT Ministry's official site shows the implementation of all its points and can be openly accessed. The IT Action Plan defines three major development areas of the IT industry:

1. *Info-Infrastructure Drive as a key factor for the industry development*: The main objective is to develop a world class information infrastructure, which provides for a 30% annual growth of the entire telecommunications infrastructure from the 1998 level that had the following performance indicators:

   — Fiber Optic communication – 75,000 km of fiber optic;

   — VSAT (Very Small Aperture Terminal) – aggregate channel capacity of over 300 . bit per second;

   — Satellite antennas – aggregate channel capacity of 3,000 . Hz.

   The program involves measures to build state-of-the-art information infrastructure, to develop and integrate local, national and global telecommunications infrastructure into a single network by developing fiber optic links, satellite telecommunication and wireless. Proposed measures to implement this include:

   — Delicensing of certain services;

   — Lower tariffs;

   — Private sector development;

   — Privatization of India's major state-owned telecommunication company – VSNL;

   — Demonopolization of international VSNL Internet outlets, development of private Internet providers for international outlets;

— Building of Hi-Tech Habitats with developed infrastructure and research/educational institutes, etc.

2. *Target ITEX-50 (ITEX – IT EXport) – to reach U.S.$ 50 billion exports by 2008. It also includes some measures to develop the domestic software and services market.*

— To this end, taxation policies have been revised , namely:

— Zero customs duty and zero excise rates on software imports were introduced from January 1, 1999;

— Phased reduction to zero of customs duty on hardware and hardware-related imports;

— Zero income tax on software and services exports for individual software developers;

Tax allowances were introduced for PC purchasers;

— 100% depreciation of hardware and software within 2 years after purchase. In terms of finances, the software and services industry was announced as a priority industry for investments, and Schemes of preferential financing for the industry's enterprises were proposed;

— Measures were taken to create favorable conditions for venture capital foundations, in particular, the withholding of corporate taxes on investments in software development companies, etc.

As part of the ITEX-50 program, measures are being taken

— To promote Indian companies in the global market;

- — To optimize investments by Indian companies in foreign firms and purchases of foreign companies' shares;
- — In the global market, to create India's image of a provider of high quality services and products;
- — To provide government support and incentives for the companies to obtain ISO 9000, IS/ISO 9000, ISO 14000, SEI CMM certifications of the 2 and higher levels;
- — To promote Indian brands, etc.

3. *Information Technology for all by 2008: informatization in all walks of lif.:* As part of this program, the following measures are being implemented:

- — National program of overall computer literacy, a broader computer park and Internet access, adjustment of imported software, software translation into the languages of nationalities residing in India.
- — Program of computerization and broad use of the Internet in all walks of life, including banking transactions, medicine, education, e-commerce, development of information centers and libraries, etc.
- — Program of IT-supported national governance and of highly effective information links to citizens.
- — Program to improve quality of IT education of all levels (from elementary to high school, graduate and postgraduate) and to train skilled IT staff. As part of this program, an ad-hoc government commission was set up within the Department of higher and secondary education in July-August

2000. It was made up of Minister of Education, Minister of Finance, IT Minister and others. The Commission adopted a program - "Human Resource Development in IT"12 . Its measures aim to raise IT education to the world's highest level, using, among others, the following ways and means:

— To improve the quality of secondary and higher IT education;

— To train highly skilled specialists using global IT technologies;

— To make specializations of trained staff more consistent with software industry requirements;

— To increase the number of IT graduates;

— To coordinate activities of the private and public education sectors;

— To organize various types of Internet education, systems of remote education and the use of PCs to improve educational levels.

India's IT Industry

In India, the government's liberal policies toward IT companies prompted a phenomenal growth of the IT industry. Since 1991, the industry's annual turnover growth has been 50% on average. In Fiscal Year (FY)1999-2000, the turnover of the IT industry was U.S.$ 8.6 billion, with software and services production amounting to U.S.$ 5.7 billion (over 66%). In the first half of FY 2000-2001, the domestic market of software and services increased by 48%, and the overall industry growth was 58%. According to Digital Planet 2000 , in 1999 India's domestic ICT market reached U.S.$ 15 billion, and against 1993 increased almost six-fold. Currently ICT spending in India as a percentage of the GNP tends to grow . While in FY 1999-2000 it was 1%, by 2003 it is projected to reach 2.5 %. At present, turnover of some Indian companies exceeds U.S.$ 100 million, the largest of them being:

— Tata Consultancy Services (TCS)– annual revenue reached U.S.$ 489 million in FY 1999-2000;

— Wipro Technologies – annual revenue reached U.S.$ 254 million in FY 1999-2000;

— Infosys Technologies – respective figure is U.S.$ 212 million within the same period.

Software Exports

Software and services exports in India are steadily growing, with annual growth rates at an average of 40% in the last two decades (1980 - 2000). Nasscom (National Association of Software and Services Companies) data shows, that in FY 1999-2000 the total software and services exports reached U.S.$4 billion (according to India's software and services exports grew by 63% and reached U.S.$ 2.86 billion, which was 13% of India's total export for these six months . During 2000-2001, software exports are expected to be worth U.S.$ 6.24 billion.

Net IT export revenues (minus staff travel expenses, marketing costs, and imports of related hardware and software, etc.) are currently estimated at 40% of the above figures. India's high IT export growth rates should also be considered against the background of the export's technological specifics typical of developing countries on the whole.

Productivity

Comparison of actual volume of work done by an Indian developer per time unit shows that Indian specialists working at their Western clients' sites achieve productivity levels as high as those of their Western counterparts and sometimes higher by 20-50%. Figures within India suggest that productivity varies quite widely from one company to another, but on the whole it achieves 90%-50% of that in the West. This can be accounted for by a number of constraints, with the most important of them being:

— Shortage of skilled managers;

— Lack of resources. Major companies well-established in the market are much less affected by these constraints due to larger funds and high technologies used to manage the engineering process. Lower labor productivity is partly compensated by a longer work week: a 45-hour week in India against a 35- or 40-hour week in the West.

Income

Total income divided by the number of employees will give one of the productivity indicators – income per head. The Indian software industry has the following indicators:

— Income per head in onsite work abroad, is roughly twice that for offshore work in India.

— Income per head in export–oriented companies is 2 or 3 times that in domestic-oriented software production.

— Income per head in software services exports is about half that for software package exports.

— Income per head in larger software companies is about twice that in smaller firms. Income per head in the wholly-owned multinational subsidiaries is the highest in the industry.

— Income per head in software exports is about one-quarter that in the U.S. software industry, which is linked to a proportion of packages in software exports and to lower wages.

Service Quality

The government and business policies targeted for better quality products and services resulted in international recognition of the Indian IT industry: by April 1, 2000, 210 companies obtained certifications ISO 9000 and SEI CMM Level 3 and higher, and about 70 were in the process of obtaining them . As of January 2001, out of 44 companies with the highest SEI CMM Level 5 certification, 24 companies are Indian, including Wipro Technologies, Tata Consultancy Services, InfoSys and others .

Investments

Between 1996 and 2000, venture capital investments in the Indian IT industry grew from U.S.$ 20 million to U.S.$ 370 million. At present the country has registered

28 venture foundations, 18 of which were registered during the year 2000. According to Nasscom, in FY 2000-2001 venture capital growth will reach 100%, which in absolute terms will come up to U.S.$ 700 million. It is remarkable that 38% of this amount is invested by non-resident Indians. In 2001-2002, investments in the industry are expected to double, and in 2008 they will reach U.S.$ 10 billion, and India will rate among the first five countries with the highest venture capital investments in the IT industry.

Businessmen of different countries – Indians by birth – are actively investing in Indian IT companies and set up their companies' branches in India. The World Bank is an active investor. Among its recent initiatives in India's IT development is the funding of the following projects:

— To improve quality of technical education,

— Telecommunications reforms.

At present, nearly all major global IT companies, including Microsoft, IBM, Cisco Systems, Lucent Technologies, Motorola and others, have their branches and centers in India and are active in their further development. For example, Motorola India Electronics Ltd. (MIEL) (a branch of Motorola, Inc.) invested U.S.$ 40 million last year to establish the largest center near the city of Bangalore. Only in the past few months:

— IBM announced its intention to open a research laboratory in India with 500 staff members;

— Nortel Networks, whose 1,300-employee center is already located in India, announced its plans to invest another U.S.$ 350 million in its development within the next three years and to increase its staff in India up to 1,800;

— Cisco Systems intends to allocate U.S.$ 200 million to develop its center in India;

— Deutsche Bank has invested U.S.$ 4.335 million to build a development center in India, with about 500 programmers.

Telecommunications

Since the mid-80s, the Indian Government has been focusing on funding and developing the country's telecommunications infrastructure. While domestic communications development still remains the government's priority area, it has also allocated funds to develop international communications required for export development.

Since 1990, government investments in domestic and international communications have annually increased by 15%. Intensive development of telecommunications infrastructure is the most important prerequisite for the industry's further development. India's largest telecommunications company – VSNL 22 (Videsh Sanchar Nigam Limited) – a monopolist (before April 1, 2002) in providing India's Internet international communications – is investing about U.S.$ 1.36 billion (59 billion Rupees) in telecommunications infrastructure development from 1997 to 2002, under a 5-year VSNL plan. Until recently India had international outlets whose aggregate channel capacity was 396. bit/sec, while the Nasscom-estimated demand was10 Gbit/sec by the end of 2000.

India can realistically attain these figures in the near future due to deep-sea FLAG channels (10 Gbit/sec) and SMW3 (Sea-Me-We-3) (another 20 Gbit/sec). Domestic telecommunications infrastructure development also enhances the number of Internet users: as of March 31, 2000, India had over 770,000 Internet subscribers, with the actual number of Internet users being estimated at 3.2 million people. According to Nasscom projections, by the end of FY 2000-2001 (by March 31, 2001) the target figure is 1.6 million people.

Software Technology Parks (STPs)

Currently there are 19 structural units of Software Technology Parks (STPs) united in a single autonomous formation by the IT Ministry – a network of Software Technology Parks of India – STPI. Basic Characteristics of India's Software Technology Parks (STP), Export Processing Zones (EPZ) and Export Oriented Units (EOU)

— Simpler export-import procedures, zero customs duties;

— A quick "single window" for all bureaucratic dealings;

— Lower sales taxes and excise rates;

— 10-year corporate tax exemption for STPs and 5-year corporate tax exemption for EPZs and EOUs;

— Simpler access to hard currency;

— Wholly owned foreign firms;

— Well-developed telecommunications infrastructure, access to international communications channels, in particular, to satellite communications;

— More vacant production premises and preferential terms to build new production facilities;

— Cash compensatory support and reduced rents of facilities, apartments, and lower prices for water and power supplies;

— A well-developed social and communal infrastructure, etc.

Currently the STPI share of software and services exports is 60%. STPs have 15 international outlets due to land-based satellite communication stations F3 IBS.

IT Professionals

According to Nasscom data, as of March 31, 2000, 340,000 professional software developers are employed in the Indian software industry, 80% of whom are Masters of Science in Engineering. According to the data of the Indian Department of Higher and Secondary Education , for the year 2000, about 68,000 specialists in computer technology annually graduate from Indian colleges and universities. Projections by the IT Ministry and the Department of Higher and Secondary Education say that by 2008 public higher educational institutions will have trained 1.79 million IT specialists, 263,000 of whom will get Master's and higher degrees, while 785,000 will get Bachelor's degrees.

The growing needs of the IT industry call for an annual increase in IT graduates: in the 1999-2000 academic year, public, budget-based higher educational institutions trained 25% more specialists than in the previous year, before 1999 the annual growth was on average 15%. The number of IT specialists trained by private universities and Master of Computer Applications courses is steadily growing. according to Nasscom, every year they have 40,000-50,000 graduates. An increasing number of IT specialists get remote education from open universities or migrate to the IT industry from related hi-tech branches, which is an additional significant source of employees.

India developed a network of Institutes of Information Technologies, including IIIT (Indian Institute of Information Technology) and IIT (Institute of Information Technology), located in different Indian states. All of these educational institutions have flexibly organized academic processes closely linked to production. Thus, the Indian Institute of Information Technologies (IIIT)located in the city of Hyderabad includes schools of IBM, Microsoft, Motorola, Oracle, Metamor and Satyam companies, equipped with new hi-tech equipment. Lecture courses are worked out in conformity with current IT development trends and specific needs of the companies. Great attention is given to managerial training. Training of specialists is done by academics from major U.S. universities.

High turnover rate is typical of most Indian companies: the number of employees leaving the companies ranges from 15-20% to 50% a year. Staff turnover is a major problem in their business development, and for some companies – the major problem. Some of the employees leave to work in other Indian companies, others – 10-15% - go to work or study overseas. The reason for these high losses is a chance to get a qualitatively better job, given high demand for IT specialists both at home and abroad. Considering the specifics of the contracts carried out by most Indian companies, education, experience and skills of employees remain underused. This is the reason why higher remuneration plays an important but not domineering role in changing jobs. The most important factors are:

— Involvement in more advanced, state-of-the-art projects;

— Creative self-fulfillment, involvement in project analysis and design;

— Work in a professionally challenging environment;

— Access to greater range of resources – software, hardware, etc.

The Government's targeted policies and Nasscom's efforts to protect copyrights of software producers make the share of licensed software steadily increase. Thus, according to Nasscom, 98% of the entire software in the Indian market was piratical in 1986, but by 1999 the share of licensed software grew to 40%.

According to joint survey made by Nasscom and McKinsey Global Institute , and also according to data of India's IT Ministry , with the current tendencies and the favorable economic and political climate sustained, by 2008 the software and IT services industry will play a key role in the Indian economy:

— Software and services production in India will reach U.S.$ 87 billion;

— On the whole the IT industry in India will be estimated at U.S.$ 140 billion;

— Projected minimal capitalization of the software and services market will reach U.S.$ 225 billion;

— 10 Indian transnational corporations will have annual turnover of over U.S.$ 2 billion each;

— Software and services will constitute over 7.5% of the total growth of India's GDP;

— The package software market will reach U.S.$ 18 billion, U.S. $10 billion of which will be the domestic market;

— From 2001, software and services exports will annually double and by 2008 will amount to U.S.$ 50 billion p.a.;

— 2.2 million specialists will be employed in the sector, about 200,000 of whom will be high professionals and will be involved in Class «» development – hi-tech software production, about 570,000 – in IT services and e-business;

— Foreign investments in the sector will come up to about U.S.$ 4-5 billion, which exceeds the volume of all foreign investments in the Indian economy in 1998.

Software and Services Exports

The Indian IT industry can best be described as export-oriented. India refuted a widespread opinion that IT exports require a strong national industry and a well-developed domestic market. The following specific regional features made for the development of an export-oriented software industry:

— Sufficiently large English-speaking communities (5% of the total population), and English is known to be the IT language.

— On average, very low living standards in a one-billion-people country, which creates conditions for a large market of relatively cheap labor.

— Mathematical culture, whose history in India is over 2000 years long.

In the words of Indians themselves, they are a nation of mathematicians, which is another prerequisite for hi-tech development and training of top-notch specialists. India has become successful as a software and IT services exporter due to the following important factors:

— Government officials concerned about the country's advance along this path. Established technocratic government bodies, promoting and patronizing the industry.

— Nasscom as an active and influential organization that united software companies. Nasscom has an important role to play in the industry's policy-making at different levels, including the governmental one. It was established in 1988 and consolidated 38 companies with the total revenues of 65% of the software industry. As of December 31, 2000, Nasscom comprised 797 companies whose overall revenues equaled 95% of the total revenues of India's software and IT services industry.

— Large Indian Diaspora in many countries throughout the world, and especially strong a diaspora in the U.S., where it is getting increasingly influential both economically and politically.

Importers of IT Services

Before the late 80s, the U.S. was the principal importer of India's software and services. Currently the U.S. still occupies this position. However, since 1990 a significant part of Indian IT exports has gone to other countries.

According to a Nasscom report, in 1999-2000 India exported software and services to 95 countries, with a larger portion of exports – nearly 62% – going to North America (the U.S. and Canada), 23.5% – to Europe, 3.5% – to Japan, 5% – to other Asian countries, 1.5% – to Australia and New Zealand, 4.5% – to other countries of the world.

The initiatives of the government and Nasscom which gave birth to a program of Indian-European software cooperation – NIESA (Nasscom's India Europe Software Alliance), made it possible to develop steady trade relations between India and West European countries in software and services supplies. In 1999-2000, software exports to European countries reached 23.5% (in 1997-1998 it was 20%) of the total software exports or U.S.$ 920 million, with nearly half of the European exports going to Great Britain.

European countries are becoming increasingly aware of the benefits they get from offshore project development by Indian companies. IT workforce shortages in Germany, Austria, Great Britain, France and Italy result in lowering entry visa barriers, and more and more often companies in these countries invite Indian specialists to work directly at their sites.

Japan is another important geographic area of Indian software exports. Japan is the second largest world ICT market after the U.S. For broader trade relations with Japan, Nasscom also developed a software cooperation project – NINJAS (Nasscom's India Japan Software Alliance). In 1999-2000, software and services exports to Japan amounted to about U.S.$ 140 million, with its gradual planned increase to U.S.$ 500 million by 2002-2003. In 2000 during his visit to India (the first visit by a

Japanese head of state to India since 1990), Japanese Prime Minister Yoshiro Mori visited Bangalore, in particular, the Wipro and Infosys corporate centers which have long been working for Japanese clients. The Prime Minister said that India and Japan had a great potential in IT cooperation and made a few proposals for its further development. Being increasingly recognized in the world, Indian software companies consistently expand their exports geographically. India enters into new developing markets.

IT Services Exports

India's first software export was registered in 1974. According to DoE reports and Dataquest statistics, in 1980 it reached the mark of U.S.$ 4 million. On average, annual export growth rates over the decade - from FY 1989-1990 (105.4 million) to FY 1999- 2000 constituted 42%. Software and services export in 1999-2000 reached U.S.$ 4 billion

India's IT industry is characterized by a high degree of capital concentration. According to Nasscom data for 1999-2000, out of 1,250 IT export firms:

— 37 companies exported over U.S.$ 2.3 million of software and services;

— 60 companies exported over U.S.$ 1.15 million of software and services;

— 6 firms (Tata Consultancy Services, Wipro Infotech, Infosys Technologies, Satyam, HCL Technologies and NIIT) cover over 40% of the total exports;

— Seventy percent of export revenues are earned by top 20 software companies, with

— 12 of them having the highest certification – SEI CMM Level

According to a Nasscom report, in 1999-2000, development of projects related to the Y2K problem, resulted in nearly 12% of revenues for all Indian software and services exports, which was about U.S.$ 480 million. On the whole, from 1996 to 1999 the solution of the Y2K problem injected into the Indian software industry U.S.$ 2.5 billion, however experience acquired in the process has become a much more important asset and helped build a solid basis for further partnerships with foreign clients.

Currently the Indian software industry is going through a period of global transformation and is heading for new challenges in areas related to e-commerce and IT-enabled services. It is also active in developing areas of IT services. In FY 1999-2000, India's revenues from software and services exports in e-commerce reached U.S.$ 500 million. In 2000-2001, this figure is expected to rise to U.S.$ 1.4 billion, and by 2008 to equal 20% of India's total software exports.

The second important development area in IT services, along with e-commerce, is IT-enabled services which includes organization of information telephone services, support services, database processing and support in various socio-economic sectors, World Web development, etc. The global market of IT services in this area equals U.S.$ 10 billion. In the opinion of Nasscom international consultants, this market keeps steadily growing and by 2008 will reach U.S.$ 200 billion. It is planned that about 1.3 million specialists will be employed in this Indian sector and its revenues will reach U.S.$ 17 billion. Some major Indian companies

(Wipro, NIIT and others), and also the Indian branches and centers of the world's computer giants (Microsoft, Motorola, Intel, IBM, Cisco, HP and others) are developing systems software, including those for network and embedded systems.

Initially India's IT export was dubbed "body shopping". Thus, in 1988, labor export was a domineering trend: 75% of all export earnings came from the work done by Indian specialists at the client's site overseas ('onsite'), mainly in the USA. Export share of offshore programming was only 25% of the total exports. There were no finished products (packages) from India in the world market. The situation has changed by now: 50% of exports is onsite work overseas, about 45 % is offshore programming, export of packages is no more than 5% of the total volume.

Export of Labor

India loses 15% of IT specialists annually due to immigration, mainly to the USA. About half of the U.S. work visas are issued to immigrants from India. According to the INS – the U.S. Immigration and Naturalization Service,:

About 1.5 million people of Indian origin reside in the USA. According to official statistics, the average income of an Indo-American family amounts to U.S.$ 60,093, while the average family income in the U.S. is U.S.$ 38,885. This high income reflects the high educational level of the Indian diaspora. 87% of Indian-born Americans graduated from high schools, 62% – from colleges, 58% of 25-year-old Indo-Americans received Bachelor's and higher degrees. In the Silicon Valley about

300,000 Indians work in computer companies and 7% of IT firms are headed by Indians by birth.

Here are just a few of the well-known names: one of the founders of Sun Microsystems is an Indian – Vinod Hosla; HotMail founder is also an Indian – Sabir Bhatia (he sold his company to Microsoft for U.S.$ 400 million). o In the Silicon Valley alone, 774 computer companies were established by Indians by birth, among them about 15 IT companies have an annual turnover between U.S.$ 100 million and U.S.$ 1 billion. o Over 15% of all start-up companies in the region have been established by Indians. The USA has become home for thousands of Americans of Indian origin, who are involved in the IT business and whose wealth amounts to millions of dollars. According to some data, there are over 5,000 millionaires of Indian origin in the Silicon Valley alone. Many of them made fortunes of billions of dollars: e.g. the wealth of Guriradj Deshpande, co-founder of some companies dealing with network technologies, is estimated at U.S.$ 4-6 billion.

The Indian Diaspora in the U.S. actively supports its homeland, encouraging the inflow of capital to India. Among its members are both venture capital owners investing in Indian IT companies and a great deal of immigrants from India who established their own companies or are CEOs in U.S. IT companies and contribute to a continuous flow of offshore contracts.

The professional level of Indians leaving to work abroad is much higher than the average of the Indian IT industry, which means that for some explicit and implicit reasons the best qualified specialists tend to immigrate. Work abroad on a temporary contract in many cases entails immigration, which is often seen as negative, i.e.

"brain drain", in terms of benefits to India. However, this process also has some positive implications for donor-countries supplying skilled labor:

Compared to irreversible 'domestic brain drain', i.e. inevitable loss of skills when the work has to be done at a low technological level or is not related to the skills at all, 'external brain drain' makes it possible for the specialists to get access to new state-of-the-art technologies, to improve their skills and to return home at a qualitatively new professional level. At micro-level, some software developing companies, who send their specialists to work abroad, see this as a stepping stone to penetrating into the world market. Well-reputed specialists create a positive image of their home companies and help build a zone of confidence and, by so doing, attract new clients to the national market.

All these factors contribute to the development of the national IT industry. One result of the intellectual immigration is opening branches and missions of national companies in Western countries, which, in turn, helps further promote these companies in the world market. Practically all major Indian companies have now opened their offices in the U.S., Japan, Canada, and also in some West European countries. The immigrants can create a powerful lobby for their own country to expand its presence in the IT market, to promote the growth of commercial interest to invest in the country which supplies intellectual workforce.

Thus, immigrants from India are currently employed at the managerial level of most major U.S. IT companies, which enables them to lobby the interests of Indian developers by facilitating the use of Indian companies as project developers.

The Indian Diaspora has become an influential political and economic force in the USA. Indian liberal policies and successful tactics of immigrant businessmen resulted in the emergence of many joint ventures both in the USA and in India and in a great deal of missions and full-fledged branches of U.S. companies in India.

Offshore Software Development

Terminologically, offshore software development means doing programming in countries with cheap labor for cost-efficiency purposes, and outsourcing or contract programming means delegating orders to high-class professionals when companies are unable to do the job on their own. According to the Nasscom report for FY 1999-2000, 185 of the Fortune 500 companies outsourced their projects to Indian software developers. In 2001, their number will increase to 300, and by 2003, Indian companies plan to provide these services to 80% of the Fortune 500 companies.

Software development is usually seen as broken down into the following standardized basic production stages:

— Analysis and specification of software requirements

— Design of software

— Coding/programming and testing of software

— Software installation and support

Actual software development is somewhat different from this simple picture (many processes are conducted in parallel and some iteration, etc.), this model is close enough approximation to reality, as it shows that software development has been fragmented and standardized and, thus, made into a production process. Software analysis and design are technologically the most complex (and requiring higher skills and experience) and the most expensive. Programming and testing constitute only 10-15% (by some estimation, up to 30% at the most) of the total project cost and do not require higher skills. In the international division of labor the majority of contracts allocate only the less-skilled coding and testing stage to Indian workers: 80% of all contract jobs carried out by Indians are coding, testing and support, while Western software developers carry out more skill-intensive work.

Recently there has been some tendency for change and increase in hi-tech projects. More and more companies can carry out the full life cycle development. For example, in its Indian-based research and development centers, Wipro does the entire cycle of software development for companies like Intel, Sun Microsystems, Tandem, Alcatel and Cisco. On the whole, it has become possible due to the following factors:

— Indian companies accumulated sufficient experience in organizing and realizing offshore projects, achieved coordination in client-contractor relationship that made it possible to start remote project development with software analysis and design;

— export of labor and offshore programming opened access to new technologies and advanced experience, and helped become aware of the need to train specialists (in particular, managers, analysts, and designers) and to raise education to a proper level.

Export of Packages in IT Services

Exports of packages in India's software and services exports currently constitute no more than 5%. Primarily they are adjusted software (i.e. not new but already existing software products adjusted to the needs of specific consumer groups), and also, to a much smaller degree, new packages developed for foreign companies and sold under their brands. This is a logical situation, since the export of packages requires good marketing and, hence, large investments: major companies spend 40-50% of their funds on marketing and sales. Besides, investments in R&D require 10-15% of the company's revenues.

According to Nasscom data, in 1999-2000 this figure in the Indian software industry was on average only 3.4%, which was marked progress compared to FY 1997-1998 when software companies invested in R&D 2.5% on average. Some major Indian companies have already reached the world levels of spending on technological R&D: e.g. in FY 1999-2000 Wipro invested in this business area approximately 14% of the company's total annual revenues.

However, in absolute terms, these amounts are insignificant against those of Western companies: R&D investments of only one major Western company come up to billions of dollars, which is more than the overall revenues of all Indian software producers taken together. For example, the Microsoft R&D budget is 7-10 times more than the total revenues of Tata Consulting Services (TCS) – a major Asian firm, and Microsoft spending on sales and marketing is comparable with software development revenues of continents.

Considering that only 1-5% of developed products are successful and in demand, and also that Indian companies do not have their own famous brands, the difficulties they face in the market of package exports become obvious. Yet, at present Indian companies begin to show some growth in production and export of packages. Namely, TCS exports to the world market about 14 application programs for banking and finance, insurance, medicine, etc; the Wipro corporation has developed some first-class packages – Cybermanage (network management system), Softchips (a unique system based on the semi-conducting technology developed by the company for telecommunications and other industrial spheres), etc. Thus, qualitative and quantitative growth of Indian software companies creates conditions for producing and promoting their own packages and new technologies in the world market.

Software and Services Companies

Software companies are mainly located around a few major Indian cities. Before the mid-80s, Mumbai was the center of this industry. However, since the late 80s software companies have been concentrating around Bangalore, which on the analogy with California's Silicon Valley is now called India's Silicon Plateau. These concentrations are determined by the following basic factors:

— Availability of skilled labor due to a broad network of research laboratories, educational institutes and public sector IT firms. By STPI estimations, 75,000 IT specialists currently work in Bangalore. They have been a key source of entrepreneurs, since a great deal of companies have been set up by former software specialists

— High quality of life: Bangalore benefited from its reputation for a good climate, cosmopolitanism and good social conditions of life. Besides, it is famous for its 'pub culture', which in many ways facilitates informal communication and socializing of specialists and managers of different levels: Bangalore is the locus of BAIT (Beer-Drinkers Association of Information Technology.

— Modern and extensive infrastructure. Unlike Mumbai, Bangalore has a better water and power supply and better developed transportation infrastructure.

Apart from these factors, Bangalore became Mecca of Indian software production due to one historical fact that occurred in 1986 when the U.S. company Texas Instruments (TI) set up its branch there. Later it became the first full-fledged offshore center of software development, which used satellite-based communication links to transmit data to the U.S. This was broadly reported in the home and international mass media. TI was known to have successfully cut through many red tape barriers and obstacles (particularly on imports) during its first months in India and this further encouraged firms to go to Bangalore. In FY 1999-2000, almost 400 companies located in and around Bangalore exported software and services totaling over U.S.$ 1.1 billion to the world market.

Building Software Export Sector

India's export-oriented IT industry and, in particular, extensive development of offshore programming enable the country to get access to the front line of hi-tech development and to experience in organizing industrial development of software.

The current boom in information and telecommunications technologies and globalization of world economic structures enabled India to get the recognition it deserves as a power possessing a strong scientific and technological potential as well as a source of skilled labor.

Specific regional prerequisites and the following factors provided a foundation for the dramatic growth of the Indian IT industry:

— Successful enterprise tactics, based on marketing and well-thought-out organization of production, internal and external networking, etc.

— Successful national strategy designed to promote India as an IT exporter in the global market. The Government is the industry' promoter and its policy is directed to liberalizing the industry.

-- National vision: India's success as a Third World IT colossus resulted from a thirty-year dream of businessmen and government officials alike that came true thanks to the nation's creative potential. Information technology has literally become a new mantra of Indian society.

The national strategy of the country to encourage the development of the IT industry has been implemented due to some basic initiatives undertaken by the Indian government in the following spheres:

1) Administrative Regulatory Measures:

— Delicensing of the software industry.

— Drastic simplification of registration procedures for software and services producers.

— Creation and development of government structures promoting the industry's growth (in marketing, organizing the production process, etc.).

2) Export-Import Policies

— Export incentives:

— Making tax concessions (including profit taxes) and lowering customs duties, etc. Tax exemption for software and IT services export revenues (since 1991) is worth special emphasis..

— Establishing the status of EPZs, EOUs and, especially, STPs with favorable treatments for production development.

— Introducing a 10-year tax exemption for software producing companies located in free economic zones and STPs.

3) Import liberalization:

— Gradually lowering customs duties on software imports from 114% to 0%, under the 1999 regulation.

— Introducing zero customs duties on imported textbooks, guides, operation manuals, journals and periodicals on CDs, under the1998 regulations. Lowering by stages customs duties on computer imports and computer-enabled goods.

— Introducing zero customs duties on imported computers and other equipment which after two years' use are donated to social institutions, hospitals, schools and government structures.

4) *Finances and Investments*: Incentives to attract private and foreign capital to the software industry, telecommunications infrastructure and IT education:

— Introducing tax concessions for companies, special treatment for joint ventures, private educational institutions.

— Introducing preferential lending schemes.

— Introducing schemes for risk insurances.

— 100% involvement of foreign capital in all IT areas.

— 100% involvement of foreign capital in e-commerce.

— Introducing tax concessions on purchasing shares of major foreign companies.

— Introducing tax concessions on venture capital investments in IT companies.

5) Education and Training

— Higher and secondary IT education reforms, development of a retraining system.

— Certification system for specialists.

— Incentives for standardizing education and certifying educational institutions. o Incentives for young people to get an IT education (systems of subsidies, preferential taxes, etc.).

— Incentives to attract private and foreign capital. o Government support and funding of educational institutions.

6) Telecommunications Infrastructure

— Private and foreign capital involvement in telecommunications development.

- Privatization of national telecommunications companies.
- Removal of government monopoly on various services.
- Government support and funding of telecommunications development.
- Improvements in the production process, development and introduction of advanced technologies
- Funding and crediting research and industrial hi-tech projects.
- Incentives for standardization and international certification.
- Launching a system of government contracts to encourage development and implementation of high technologies in production and management.

7) Intellectual Property Protection
   - Better legal systems and tougher punishment for breaching the intellectual property right law.
   - Economic leverage to encourage the use of licensed products.

Government's IT Policy

Since 1986, when the software sector was declared a priority area of the Indian economy, the Indian Government has been focusing on formulating a specific IT policy. The Government policy aimed to solve fundamental problems affecting the industry's development. These problems are:

— Limited capital market;

— Limited access to advanced technologies;

— Difficulties in harmonizing client-producer relations;

— Poor marketing;

— Deficiencies in the educational and training systems, etc.

A great deal of restrictions and barriers have led to:

— Somewhat lower growth rates of the software industry;

— A shift in emphasis from package production to services;

— Priority development of export production rather than the domestic market;

— More favorable conditions for major company development.

India's position in the world in the capacity of a supplier of skilled IT labor, and also of rather cheap low-tech programming. The Indian Government used a flexible iteration approach by analyzing the results of the measures taken and modifying its policies to meet the industry's changing needs. The following are some areas of further government policy improvements:

— To introduce additional financial procedures to regulate the work of the industry's companies and to promote their favorable development;

— To support private IT education, and also R&D in the private sector of the IT industry;

— To train industry-oriented staff in the system of public education;

— To develop infrastructure and to make it cheaper;.

— To develop marketing at the government level in order to promote IT companies in the global market;

— To be more active in the policies against piracy;

— To further develop the system of government contracts on software development and IT services by Indian firms;

— To make bureaucratic procedures faster and simpler, etc.

6

Assessment of the ICT Services

Today's accelerating rate of technological change, and the social, economic and cultural changes that follow in its wake, have stretched existing institutions and the fabric of society to their limits, even in the most developed societies and the strongest organisations. Many argue that technological innovations, particularly from the Information and Communications Technology (ICT) sector, are the main drivers of these changes. Others speak of an emerging 'knowledge society' as the fundamental cause. For countries in the developing world, like South Africa, this phenomenon can either be faced with pessimism and paralysis, or welcomed as an opportunity for long-overdue transformation and for the development of equitable participation in the global economy. The National Research and Technology Foresight (NRTF) project is intended to facilitate the latter approach, applying several long-range planning exercises to shape research and technology policy and to facilitate the growth of a flexible, adaptive culture of foresight throughout all sectors of society. The processes used by and the outputs and recommendations of the NRTF ICT sector working group (SWG).

How the SWG set about defining its mandate and scope by using the background of the technology scans to define a mission and a set of sector foci. The identification of sector foci was followed by an initial ICT Strengths, Weaknesses, Opportunities and Threats (SWOT) analysis. Early in the process it became clear that ICT is a cross-cutter for most other areas of importance in the SA economy, and that human resource development is a cross-cutter in all areas of ICT. A strong underlying factor to emerge from the SWOT analysis was that an aggressive national ICT vision is urgently needed to counteract obstructive policies, uncoordinated efforts, a lack of funding, inadequate skills and training, and the absence of a culture that fosters the development and effective use of ICT.

Assessment of the ICT Sector

The ICT Sector Working Group's activities to clearly define its mandate and the scope of its work for the rest of the Foresight Process. Based on the shared understanding gained from the International and Local Scans, the SWG defined their mission and finalised the sector foci. This prepared the way for the first ICT Strengths, Weaknesses, Opportunities and Threats (SWOT) analysis.

The ICT SWG will develop a long-term vision and strategy aimed at using ICT to—

— Empower all South Africans by providing equitable, interactive access to the knowledge society;

— Promote South Africa as an Africa-oriented, global ICT player through a balanced approach to private sector growth and socio-economic development;

— Provide foresight guidance that will transcend current ICTs;

— Identify those key ICTs that have the potential to help create the desired futures and provide guidelines for their development, acquisition and implementation; and

— Identify key areas for appropriate technology transfer and HR development.

The ICT SWG was challenged by the growing, and very broad, impact of ICT across all sectors of society. In many ways, ICT can be seen as a cross-cutter rather than a separate sector. An ICT industry can be identified, but cognisance must be taken of new components needing to be added because of technology convergence driven by digitisation. In addition, all aspects of the role ICT can and will play as an empowerment tool across all sectors of society need to be recognised. A consultative process to define the sector was conducted to crystallise the sector boundary conditions to enable the SWG to focus its work. Some preliminary meetings to discuss the main foci and priority functional areas of the sector were held in several main centres throughout the country. In light of the outputs of these meetings, and after analysis of the International and Local ICT Scans, the SWG selected the following foci:

Within five years, broad-bandwidth infrastructure is expected to be cheaply available, even to remote and disadvantaged areas. Focus is needed on—

— the 'last mile', via appropriate alternative technologies and power supplies (e.g. wireless and solar power);

— the opportunities and flexibility provided by the convergence of technologies driven by digitisation;

— developing Research and Technology (R&T) capabilities to handle emerging technologies rather than perpetuating legacy infrastructure.

As economies move from the Industrial paradigm to the Knowledge paradigm, ICT will have a growing impact on the learning and development of individuals and organisations, and on the need for flexible employment and employability. Focus is needed on—

— needs-driven, ICT-facilitated, virtual learning 'anywhere, anytime, anyway' for all ages, and across all sectors of society;

— ICT as an employment maker rather than a job taker, and its role in the 'brain drain';

— developing R&T capabilities in learning processes (individual and organisational), enhanced by ICT.

Growing the ICT industry

With a few exceptions, South Africa's ICT Industry is fairly stagnant, often dependent on legacy technologies. Focus is needed on—

— dramatic improvements in ICT literacy, skills, training, education and R&T across all sectors of society;

— developing globally competitive software and hardware capabilities, particularly to satisfy the needs of the African Renaissance and the developing world;

— the role of ICT and related R&T in accelerating the growth of the SMME sector.

The accelerating rate of ICT innovation in the international arena requires that South Africa identify niche areas within which to compete, and develop R&D clusters and the necessary open markets to nurture 'co-opetition' type relationships with international partners. Focus is needed on—

— developing a strategy for identifying specific ICT opportunities and positioning the local industry for competitive innovation, as part of an ongoing foresighting process;

— safeguarding intellectual property rights (IPR), particularly as they apply to indigenous knowledge;

— the financial, human resource, and regulatory aspects of developing capacity for basic technology development, and for taking this all the way through to products/services;

— the use of ICT to lower barriers of entry into other R&D areas.

As a major, but unimaginative, user of ICT, the public sector needs to rapidly streamline its operations to make far better use of ICT, and to make wiser use of its influence as a dominant consumer of ICT products. Focus is needed on—

— a national ICT strategy, including policy for promoting local R&T, for positioning South Africa for innovation and for technical development in ICT;

— applications aimed at producing order-of-magnitude improvements in the delivery of health, housing, crime prevention, and other government services;

— the emergence of an ICT literate civil service, and an ICT-facilitated open democracy.

Access to ICT and social issues

The tendency of ICT to widen the gap between the already empowered haves and

— the marginalised have-nots is particularly evident in South Africa. Focus is needed on

— the diffusion of technology throughout society to create a national ICT culture, to the extent that it should have an effect on the voluntary reversal of urbanisation;

— appropriate human/computer interfaces which address the cultural and language diversities of the country, and the common ICT phobias of marginalised people;

— partnerships with foreign technology developers aimed at influencing and contributing to the appropriateness of technology for South Africa, and finding a workable balance between multinational business interests and local socio-economic development.

Infostructure for the individual and organisation

South Africa has moved rapidly, along with the rest of the world, towards a knowledge society in which information is the most marketable class of product and individual capabilities transcend corporate structures. Focus is needed on—

— infostructure to nurture emerging digital communities (digital libraries, virtual information, entertainment and infotainment hubs, on-line government, e-commerce and on-line marketing, and virtual reality), and promote a large ICT-empowered middle class;

— reliable and socially acceptable mechanisms (across the cultural spectrum) for data security, privacy and integrity;

— specific technologies which allow digital communities to resist non-ICT influences which work against their formation (security systems, telemedicine, teleworking, distance education);

— organisational restructuring facilitated by ICT innovations;

International (Regional/Global) ICT issues

South Africa is a follower of global ICT trends and adopts technology largely because of aggressive marketing, as opposed to the attractiveness and appropriateness of the product. To a lesser extent, South Africa's neighbours are forced to follow South Africa's ICT decisions. Focus is needed on—

— emergence of world (including regional) collaboration on global regulations and standards, with a significant voice given to the growing developing world market (e-commerce, distance education, global network management, content creation);

— investment in international ICT ventures in order to become an influential global player;

— making South Africa attractive (tax incentives, security, a culture of ICT innovation) for digital skills, migration to happen in both directions, and recognising emerging global lifestyle trends early (citizen of the world via ICT);

— a strong national ICT strategy, which has explicit linkages between political leaders (representing ownership and stakeholders) and ICT policies as they affect the emerging knowledge society, and which coordinates initiatives and responses to global ICT processes;

During this analysis, the SWG repeatedly emphasised that South Africa needs urgently to formulate an appropriate and broadly supported national ICT vision to underpin all of the above focus areas, key components of which should be—

— the development of HR across the ICT sector, which is essential to the economic survival of South Africa. The national plan should concentrate upon harnessing the potential of the youth of the country, and should aim to achieve a net inflow of brainpower in the medium term (five to ten years);

— the formulation of collaborative ventures which balance multinational and national interests;

— the identification of national needs and priorities;

— the creation of a national culture conducive to ICT innovation and to rapid adaptation to new technologies.

Stakeholders: In preparation for the SWOT analysis, the SWG agreed that it would add value to consider the key stakeholders, including beneficiaries (direct, indirect, and potential), customers, and clients. The following groups were identified:

Key stakeholders

— Government (National, Provincial, Local)

— Private sector (local - including SMMEs - and multinationals)

— Previously and currently disadvantaged people (80%+ of population)

— Labour

— NGOs + civil society

— Empowered individuals (including the 'connected' elite)

— ICT industry

— The international community (IFAs, the UN, ITU, WTO, etc.) The SWG's shared understanding of the main issues under each focus area was then expanded by evaluating their impacts on each of the above stakeholder groups in terms of their social, technological, environmental, economic, political and values contexts (i.e. a STEEPV analysis).

A combination of national commitment and licence obligations imposed by government is driving an accelerated rollout of telecommunications infrastructure. This is complemented by a competent (though far too small) existing skills base, and the enthusiasm and desire amongst the youth of the country to acquire ICT knowledge. South Africa enjoys a culture of rapid ICT uptake. Having English as the country's common language of communication is a distinct advantage in the international ICT field. Since 1994, the government has followed a path of consultation and accountability, culminating in a Freedom of Information Bill with ICT as the enabling technology. Several initiatives are under way to leverage public service delivery through ICTs. The existing ICT infrastructure in the country is effective; SA is amongst the world's top twenty countries for Internet connectivity. Telkom's backbone, and the ICT capacity in financial institutions, the tertiary education sector, the CSIR, and other former statutory organisations, are very good on the whole, particularly in relation to the rest of Africa.

South Africa is the African leader for ICT vision, skills and facilities. International ICT links are continually strengthening, and many multinationals see South Africa as the springboard into Africa. The move towards improving the ICT infrastructure and providing universal access is having a positive impact on the economy.

Large areas of the country still have minimal ICT infrastructure, and even with the falling cost of infrastructure many people cannot afford to participate in the information society. Telkom's temporary monopoly prevents competitors from speeding up service delivery. No national strategy is in place for ICT, and there is a proliferation of uncoordinated projects. The literacy and educational base in the country is very weak and skewed, and this has a direct effect on the production of scientists, engineers and ICT workers. The result is an extreme skills shortage in the ICT sector, exacerbated by the brain drain to foreign countries. ICT has created élite communities within the already skewed SA society.

The government suffers from many problems which manifest themselves in poor service delivery, and this also extends to public service ICT roll-out. Historical baggage in many forms (management, bureaucracy, policy) hampers the rapid establishment of information-based businesses. The local ICT market is small and has to operate without economies of scale. South Africa has a poor record of technology transfer from multinationals to local operations, and from universities to industry. South Africa is weak internationally in influencing global ICT policy and international standards, and is not competitive in translating international trends into 'on-the-ground' roll-out. Inadequate incentives for international investors, lack of local skills and crime limit the finances available for ICT ventures, which result in less local development and poorer local economies of scale.

There is growing evidence of a possible emerging Information Society in South Africa:

— Accelerated roll-out of ICTs as a result of falling cost.

— Licence obligations of carriers.

— The availability of new technologies.

A realisation within the developed world that major future ICT markets are in the developing countries. The development and implementation of appropriate policies, and the local propensity to become rapid adopters of technology, will accelerate the development of an Information/Knowledge Society. Through access to the information society, many new methods of education and training become possible. Government policies and legislation should provide a stimulus for the development of ICTs in the country. Then Vice-President Mbeki's office set an example for this in the years 1994 to 1999. Access to ICTs will speed up public service delivery and enhance quality. The use of ICTs could transform government. Deregulation provides an opportunity for improvement through competition, and the outsourcing of public sector contracts is an opportunity for the private sector. The reasonably strong local ICT industry and a local grasp of the problems of developing nations provide an opportunity for niche software development. The needs of smaller communities, sensitivity to multilingualism, new human-computer interfaces and translation software are examples. The Internet affords the opportunity of promoting indigenous knowledge globally. There is less investment in and reliance on older legacy systems than in developed countries.

Regional and global ICT manufacturing hubs will provide the economies of scale that are needed by exporting to African and global markets. South Africa's image as the ICT leader in Africa affords various opportunities for attracting international partnerships, influencing global ICT policy, attracting foreign investment, and promoting skills pools that transcend national boundaries. Various opportunities exist for financing ICT development in SA: the creation of an investor-friendly environment, the falling cost of ICTs, the purchasing clout of the government requiring collateral investment from contract winners, and a well-developed banking sector. SMMEs are the future of the ICT industry and many opportunities exist for their formation. Greater work environment flexibility can be created as people adopt teleworking and virtual teams are able to work around the clock. ICTs can help to bring down levels of crime and enhance security and safety.

The gap between the information haves and the unwired have-nots is exacerbated by the accelerated adoption of ICTs. The labour force is small, and generally inappropriately skilled to benefit from the knowledge era. Retraining is essential, but difficult to implement in reality. The cost of education is escalating, whilst government is faced with severe budget constants. Current distance education methodologies are largely untested in mass markets, and there is a lack of feedback from learners.

Strengths

— Accelerated roll-out of infrastructure

— Education and learning in the ICT field

— Existing skills base in place

— English - ICT's lingua franca

— Government will to introduce ICT-facilitated Public Sector services

— Existing ICT infrastructure

— ICT costs are relatively low

— South Africa's ICT leadership in Africa

— South Africa's international ICT links

— ICT is a new driver of the economy

The government is generally inefficient, and the slow rate at which policies are implemented is inappropriate for the fast-moving ICT sector. The levels of ICT literacy in the Public Sector are far too low. The effects of government downsizing and privatisation will be a worsened redundancy problem for inappropriately skilled workers.

Globalisation could easily lead to the world information society being skewed to the needs and character of the developed world. The high rate of redundancy of ICTs and globalisation expose South Africa to the threat of technology dumping by developed countries. The declining value of our currency and a local culture of non-payment in respect of services and taxes are major threats to economic growth in a global information society.

Weaknesses

— Inequitable qccess

— Lack of a national ICT strategy

— Low levels of literacy and education

— Inadequate ICT skills base, worsened by the brain drain

— ICT 'phobia' and élitism

— Poor government services hamper ICT roll-out

— Industrial age management is still being used in the ICT age

— Small local ICT market

— Poor technology transfer

— International lack of clout in ICT

— Poor conditions for investors

— ICT precipitated antisocial behaviour

New forms of social threats arise out of an untrammelled information age: invasion of privacy, increased marginalisation of sections of society, new forms of social control and new forms of crime.

South Africa, with a small but strong existing skills base and infrastructure and a relatively high international profile and GDP, is well positioned to take advantage of niche opportunities to develop a software development industry and an emerging ICT-empowered middle class. However, the threatening problems of the skills flight and the existing social barriers to ICT access, particularly the low levels of literacy and education of the vast majority of the population, present serious obstacles to this objective.

Opportunities

— Emerging information society
— Accelerated roll-out of telecommunications infrastructure
— Policies to foster an information society
— ICT enabled learning/education/training
— Distance education
— National policy to stimulate ICT development
— Public service delivery through ICT
— Transformation of government use of ICTs
— Software development to address developing world problems
— Indigenous knowledge exported via ICTs
— Less legacy infrastructure than the developed world
— International links solve several ICT weaknesses

— Various ways of financing ICT operations
— SMMEs, the future of the ICT industry
— Work patterns are more flexible
— ICTs can enhance security and safety

Threats

— ICT worsens disparities in the information society
— Lack of ICT skills in the labour force
— Education funding is low
— Distance education is not a mature medium
— Government inefficiencies - too sluggish for the fast moving ICT sector
— Government policies may lead to job losses
— Redundant and inappropriate technologies
— Globalisation favours the developed world
— A weak economy is further threatened in a global information society
— New social problems arise

The ICT Sector-specific Scenarios

In a world of ever-accelerating change, long-term strategic planning and sound decision-making need to be based on a clear and reasoned consideration of a range of possible futures. Despite realising that the future is 'unknowable', we continue to view it through the blinkers of the present. Scenario Thinking is a powerful tool that provides a systematic and imaginative way of preparing for a future beyond the paradigms of the present. Scenario thinking involves the production of multiple, rich stories that extrapolate from present reality, but assume unpredictability, challenge conventional wisdom, clarify risks and opportunities and encourage creativity and responsiveness. Scenarios reveal what could happen, not what will or should happen. They should not be confused with the still commonly used forecasting methods, which assume predictability, conceal risks and foster inertia and reactivity through single-line, impoverished projections. To ensure their usefulness, scenarios should be—

- relevant: illuminating current circumstances and concerns, and linking into current mental models;
- emergent: challenging current paradigms, and making the invisible visible;
- plausible: logical and fact-based, improving systemic understanding;
- clear: memorable and distinct alternative hypotheses.

Besides helping nations or communities see the future with different eyes, scenarios have helped to position leading corporations of the world such as Royal Dutch Shell.12 It is in this light that the National Research and Technology Foresight (NRTF) project decided to incorporate scenario planning as a crucial part of South Africa's strategic research and technology processes.

Foresight macroscenarios

Four macroscenarios depicting a wide variety of possible futures for South Africa unfolding by 2020 were developed in early 1998 by a carefully selected working group. These are published in full in a separate report obtainable from DACST which includes more details of the processes used. The macroscenarios are summarised below.

Frozen revolution macroscenario

Behind all the sound and fury, the non-implementation of government policy intended for socio-economic upliftment leaves the masses dissatisfied and key players fragmented and individually focused. Some socio-political characteristics are given below:

— Government is not a significant player either regionally or globally;

— There are several social development plans but no delivery because of policy paralysis;

— There is no national identity;

— There is no consideration of environmental sustainability;

— Indigenous knowledge systems are unsupported.

Economic characteristics

— Reactive economic policy with markets partially open, but a non-strategic approach;

— Foreign investment limited to fluid assets;

— Initial economic growth less than 2%, and shrinks to -4%;

— Economic model remains driven by primary resources.

readiness subindexes, and illustrates the basic concept behind the NRI that a nation's readiness is determined by the degree to which technology permeates across all three stakeholders of the community-individuals, businesses, and government.

Individual readiness measures the readiness of a nation's citizens to utilize and leverage ICT. Factors that are used to measure this include literacy rates, mode and locus of access to the Internet, and the degree of connectivity of individuals. The top three positions on individual readiness go to Finland, Singapore, and Iceland. Korea, at 6th place, has an exceptional score on individual readiness-the country has both high penetration of the Internet in general, and one of the highest penetrations of broadband in the world. Business readiness measures the readiness of a cross section of businesses to participate in and benefit from ICT. The aim is to focus not just on the largest corporations, but to also include small- and medium-sized businesses and their willingness to exploit ICT and invest in the ICT skills of their employees. Not surprisingly, the United States has 1st place for business readiness; it is followed by Finland, Israel, and Sweden. Also noteworthy is India's ranking of 27 for business readiness compared to its position of 70 for individual readiness; this indicates a growing digital divide between the different ICT stakeholders in the country.

Government readiness measures the readiness of a government to employ ICT. It is reflected in the policymaking machinery and internal processes of the government, and in the availability of government services online. If the polity of a nation decides to make ICT a priority, this becomes visible in the short- and long-term policy measures and laws that help encourage

ICT deployment and use. It is also apparent in the government itself using ICT and equipping its people to do the same. Singapore leads on government readiness, followed by Taiwan and Finland. Of note is Estonia, which at 13th in government readiness, an indication of the government's push in ICT; government readiness is one of the factors contributing to Estonia's overall rank of 24.

Usage

The usage component is a measure of the level of impact that ICT has had on the principal stakeholders in the NRI Framework-that is, individuals, businesses, and governments. The assessment of usage includes changes in behaviors and lifestyles, and changes in other economic and noneconomic factors brought about by the adoption of ICT. One can observe variances in country performance across the three subindexes, reflecting uneven effects across the three principal stakeholders. For example, Germany is ranked high for business usage (1st), but relatively low for individual (17th) and government (20th) usage. Another notable example is Estonia, with high government readiness (13th) and usage (8th), but relatively low positions for individual (28th) and business (31st) usage.

Individual usage gives an indication of the level of adoption and usage of ICT by a nation's citizens. This information is generated by assessing the deployment of connectivity-enhancing technologies such as telephones and Internet connections, the levels of Internet usage, and money spent online. Individual usage rankings differ significantly from rankings of individual readiness. The top performers in individual usage are Korea, Finland, Denmark, the Netherlands, and Sweden. Korea and the Netherlands stand out, as they are ranked significantly lower for both the overall NRI and overall usage. Business usage measures the level of deployment and use of ICT across all businesses in a nation. Business usage is measured by factors such as the level of business-to-business and business-to-consumer e-commerce, the use of ICT for activities such as marketing, and levels of online transactions. The top five performers are Germany, Sweden, the United States, Finland, and Iceland. Government usage is the level of use of ICT by the government of a given country.

The government, besides making ICT a priority, can also benefit from the usage of ICT itself. This usage can help the government streamline services to its citizens and improve its overall functioning. Factors used to measure this usage include the volume of transactions that businesses have with governments and the presence of government services online. The top-ranking countries on this measure are Finland, Singapore, Iceland, Taiwan, and Sweden. Of note is Estonia at 8th place, reflecting the fact that the country's government is 'walking the talk'-both promoting ICT in the country, and also using ICT for its own functioning.

Understanding E-Readiness

The degree of a nation's networked readiness is the result of a multitude of effects. There are more than 130 different variables or indicators for evaluating networked readiness, and these were narrowed down by statistical analysis to a set of sixty-four variables. These sixty-four variables were grouped under the nine subindexes of the NRI Framework. This provides us with an opportunity to study some of the interrelationships across the variables and the components/subindexes of the NRI Framework.

Any attempt to use a single measure to approximate networked readiness would be a simplification. One of the most intuitive and appealing measures that one may be tempted to use as a proxy is the GDP per capita of a country. A closer look at the NRI results would show that Estonia, with a GDP per capita of US$10,066, has an NRI score of 4.69 and is ranked 24th overall; however, Mauritius, with a very similar GDP per capita of US$10,017 has a score of 3.44 and an overall ranking of 56. There is thus a wide spread in the NRI score for a given GDP purchasing power parity (PPP) per capita; this is but one of many such examples. Nevertheless, one could look at the relationship between the NRI and GDP in order to obtain a better understanding of trends, and also to identify over—and underperformers with respect to the trend. The partial log regression plot presents a possible trend. One would immediately notice the following:

1. For a given GDP PPP per capita, there is a spread in the NRI scores around the regression plot as presented above
2. The impact of GDP seems to be very high at low GDP values, and the NRI score increases rapidly with small increases in GDP
3. Around a GDP per capita of US$9,000, the curve tapers off and the effect of increasing GDP is much less pronounced. Countries widely distanced from the regression plot could be examples of

underperformers or overperformers. Thus, Luxembourg, with a very high GDP per capita, has a moderate NRI score, whereas Finland with about half the GDP per capita of Luxembourg leads the NRI ranking. Similarly, India would be overperforming on its NRI score with respect to its GDP per capita.

Plotting ICT spending versus NRI gives a similar trend to that of GDP PPP per capita versus NRI. It is notable, however, that there is a very large spread in the NRI score at a given ICT expense (as a percentage of GDP); this raises the question of whether or not the ICT dollar is effectively promoting networked readiness. For example, Spain spends less on ICT (as a percentage of GDP) than Vietnam, but has a significantly higher score on the NRI. This emphasizes the importance of other variables (such as market and regulatory factors); these variables play a significant role in determining the degree of networked readiness of a nation.

One could be tempted to use the number of Internet users in a country as a proxy estimate of the networked readiness of a country. One would thus see the existence of a possible relationship between these, represented by the partial logarithmic regression plot. One sees that readiness scores increase sharply from 0 to 20 Internet users per 100, and much more gradually thereafter. The relatively flat curve at above 20 to 30 Internet users per 100 persons implies the importance of other factors beyond this point in influencing the degree of readiness of a nation, factors such as the quality of connectivity, speed of connectivity, and the availability of online services, among others. Interesting observations that can be made from analyzing this plot are:

— Singapore, with one of the highest Internet users per 100 persons ratio, outperforms the trend line with the highest readiness component index scores. Apart from a high concentration of businesses and the presence of a skilled workforce, Singapore benefits from a strong government push in ICT.

— Korea, with the second highest number of Internet users, performs relatively moderately on the readiness component index-the country is at 12th place, despite having one of the best broadband penetration in the world. Korea shows higher readiness on the individual dimension compared with their business and government readiness.

— India and China, with relatively low numbers of Internet users, have relatively higher readiness scores; this is probably because of the regional and demographic digital divides in these countries.

— A number of South American countries, such as Nicaragua and Uruguay, are only just starting to witness the propagation of the Internet; this is reflected in lower readiness scores.

One would expect the readiness and usage scores of a nation to move hand in hand. A country having a high degree of readiness would be able to transform this ICT capability into usage statistics, and hence show a high score on the usage component index. For example, Singapore and Finland have among the highest readiness component index scores, and this readiness is translated into real ICT usage and represented by high usage scores. A closer look at the trend of readiness versus usage at lower values of readiness will reveal that usage remains rather flat with initial increases in readiness. This leads us to believe that there is a threshold to readiness; a country needs to have a certain level of readiness with regards to ICT before there can be effective usage of and a consequent impact from ICT. A certain critical mass in terms of numbers of users, or the availability of narrowband and broadband services or of services online, is essential before these indicators are reflected in real usage metrics. Thus it can be determined that:

1. Haiti, with a readiness score of 2.19 and a low usage score of 2.19, must develop its readiness before usage starts increasing significantly;
2. Romania is a significant underperformer below the threshold level, and while it has a readiness score of 3.35, this does not result in a correspondingly higher usage level;
3. Panama and Argentina are at the threshold level;
4. Argentina, however, is a significant overperformer, with a usage level of 3.84.

Measuring a country's networked readiness remains a signifi cant challenge, and any framework or model representing networked readiness remains, at best, a simplified representation of reality. The overall NRI is a summary measure of a nation's ability to participate in and benefit from ICT. The NRI provides guidance to business leaders and public policymakers to enhance the impact of ICT on all key stakeholders-individuals, businesses, and governments.

The essence of networked readiness extends beyond any single metric; that said, there are over- and underperforming countries-countries that have put ICT on the national agenda and have strived to make it an area of excellence, and others that have not done so. The former countries have succeeded in going beyond individual measures of national income or national ICT spending to provide an optimal environment for ICT development, thus promoting high levels of readiness and usage for all three key stakeholders. Finland, Singapore, and Korea are such leaders; these three could serve as role models for other nations in their quest for ICT excellence. The NRI allows a nation to benchmark its ICT performance and determine the effectiveness of policy. It also permits a country to learn from the policy and performance of other countries with similar profiles, and to identify best practice. ICT is the key to the evolution of our practices in many domains, such as education, work, personal relations, work effectiveness, and national productivity. An interesting characteristic of ICT, such as that of the Internet and mobile communications, is that overall value increases nonlinearly with the number of connected individuals and organizations. Increasing developing countries' levels of participation in ICT not only creates benefits for these countries; it also increases the overall potential of all connected stakeholders to realize value.

Bibliography

Bjorn-Anderson, N. and Numford, E. (eds)., *Information Society*, North-Holland, 1982.

Burns, T. and Stalker, G. *The Management of Innovation* (2nd edn.). Tavistock, 1968.

Butler, Gathorne. *Organisation and Management*, Prentice Hall, 1986.

Earl, Michael. *Management Strategies for Information Technology*, Prentice Hall, 1989.

Franken, H., *et al.*, *Information Technology and the Law*, Lelystad (Netherlands): Koninklijke Verrmande, 1991.

Galliers, R. 'Information systems and technology planning within a competitive strategy framework', in *Information Management. State of the Art Report*, P. Griffiths (ed.), Pergamon, 1986.

Halevi G., *The Role of Computers in Manufacturing Processes*, John Wiley, New York, 1982.

Lloyd Andrew, "Europe Examines Electronic Democracy", New Scientist, June 2, 1983. On Council of Europe report, *New Possibilities for Democratic Participation Resulting From Information and Communication Technology*, Brussels, 1983.

Marshall Rose T, *The simple book: an introduction to management of TCP/IP internet*, London, Prentice-Hall, 1991.

McLeod, Raymond, *Management Information Systems*. SRA, 1983.

Parsons, G. L. 'Information technology: a new competitive weapon', *Sloan Management Review*, Autumn 1983.

Pool Ithiel de Sola, *Technologies of Freedom: On Free Speech in an Electronic Age* Harvard University Press, Cambridge, MA, 1983.

Simons G. L., *Privacy in the Computer Age* NCC, Manchester, England, 1982.

Slack, Jennifer D., and Fred Fejes, eds. *The Ideology of Information Age*. Norwood, N. J.: Ablex, 1987.

Stewrt, V. *Change: The Challenge for Management*, McGraw-Hill, 1983.

Vincent Mosco, *The Pay-Per Society: Computer and Communications in the Information Age* (Norwood, N. J.: Ablex Publishing Co., 1989).

Winch Graham (ed.), *Information Technology in manufacturing Processes*, Rossendale, London, 1983.

Index